TEACHER EDITION

DECIMALS

USING LEGO® BRICKS

Dr. Shirley Disseler

Decimals Using LEGO® Bricks—Teacher Edition

Copyright ©2019 by Shirley Disseler
Published by Brigantine Media/Compass Publishing
211 North Avenue, St. Johnsbury, Vermont 05819

Cover and book design by Anne LoCascio
Illustrations by Curt Spannraft
All rights reserved.

Your individual purchase of this book entitles you to reproduce these pages as needed for your own classroom use only. Otherwise, no part of this book may be reproduced or utilized in any way or by any means, electronic or mechanical, including photocopying, recording, or information storage or retrieval system, without prior written permission from the publisher. Individual copies may not be distributed in any other form.

Brigantine Media/Compass Publishing
211 North Avenue
St. Johnsbury, Vermont 05819
Phone: 802-751-8802
Fax: 802-751-8804
E-mail: neil@brigantinemedia.com
Website: www.compasspublishing.org
www.brickmath.com

LEGO®, the LEGO® logo, and the Brick and Knob configurations are trademarks of the LEGO® Group, which does not sponsor, authorize, or endorse this book. All information and visual representations in this publication have been collected and interpreted by its author and do not represent the opinion of the LEGO® Group.

ORDERING INFORMATION
Quantity sales
Special discounts for schools are available for quantity purchases of physical books and digital downloads.
For information, contact Brigantine Media at the address shown above or visit
www.brickmath.com

Individual sales
Brigantine Media/Compass Publishing publications are available through most booksellers.
They can also be ordered directly from the publisher.
Phone: 802-751-8802 | Fax: 802-751-8804
www.compasspublishing.org
www.brickmath.com
ISBN 978-1-9384068-0-5

CONTENTS

Introduction 5

How to Teach with the Brick Math Series 10

Chapter 1: Introducing Decimals 13

Chapter 2: Ordering Decimals 21

Chapter 3: Fraction Equivalents of Decimals 28

Chapter 4: Decimals as Money and Time 34

Chapter 5: Adding and Subtracting Decimals 41

Chapter 6: Multiplying Decimals 54

Chapter 7: Dividing Whole and Mixed Numbers by Decimals Using a Grid Model 67

Chapter 8: Dividing Whole and Mixed Numbers by Decimals Using a Place Value Model 78

Chapter 9: Dividing by Decimals Using a Grid Covering Strategy ... 86

Chapter 10: Linking Decimals, Fractions, and Percentages 95

Appendix 103

- Suggested Brick Inventory
- Student Assessment Chart
- Baseplate Paper

DEDICATION

Dedicated to all students in middle and elementary school who struggle with the concepts of decimals. Playing leads to learning, so I hope this helps students build not only their understanding of decimals, but a love of math!

INTRODUCTION

Decimal concepts are a natural extension of the number system concepts that students learn in early elementary grades. In teaching decimals, you might first ask students the question: "What is a decimal?" While preparing to write this book, I asked this question of 100 elementary students between the ages of 6 and 12. Some of the answers were quite comical. One student stated, "A decimal is something used by grown-ups to show money." Another stated that "a decimal is part of a big number." When asked for further explanation, the student said that "'deci' means 10, so a decimal is a number divided into 10 parts." It is helpful to know students' preconceptions about the connections between whole numbers, fractions, and decimals, so that they can be corrected in the process of teaching.

The ability to understand and interpret decimals is an important life skill, relevant to activities such as making and reading measurements, calculating distances, and understanding sports statistics (Van de Walle et al., 2013). A wide range of occupations, including nursing, pharmacy work, and aeronautics, all utilize decimals.

Van de Walle, John A., Karen S. Karp, and Jennifer M. Bay-Williams. *Elementary and Middle School Mathematics: Teaching Developmentally*. Pearson Education, 2016.

While decimals are sometimes assumed to be irrelevant to early elementary students, these concepts can, in fact, be taught as early as first grade. Many early math topics relate to decimal concepts, including place value, addition and subtraction of money, and fractional parts of a whole. Students often struggle with decimals in the same way that they struggle with fractions. This is due, in part, to the fact that fraction and decimal instruction tends to jump directly into the computational aspects of addition, subtraction, multiplication, and division instead of allowing time for conceptual understanding to develop. It is also due to the fact that fractions and decimals are often taught as separate topics, rather than one integrated topic. A fraction is a form of notation used to represent the partitioning of materials into parts. A decimal is also a form of notation used to represent partitioning of materials into parts: decimal numbers are the numerator of the equivalent fraction, whose denominator is a power of ten.

Students in upper elementary grades and early middle school spend significant time exploring decimals. They should begin by linking decimals to the place values of whole numbers, which will lead to a better understanding of scientific notation. It is helpful to use a diagram, such as Table 1 below, to show the value of numbers in terms of powers of ten.

Table 1: Place Value

Hundreds	Tens	Ones	Tenths	Hundredths	Thousandths
10^2	10^1	10^0	10^{-1}	10^{-2}	10^{-3}
100	10	1	0.1	0.01	0.001

Once students understand how decimals relate to whole number place value, they can use real-world decimal models to explore this concept. Money is the most logical tool to use with students as they begin to learn how addition, subtraction, multiplication, and division work in this notation format. This process can begin when students first learn about money in early elementary school, if teachers lay the foundation for decimals by teaching students what part of a dollar is represented by pennies, nickels, dimes, and quarters (i.e., how many of each coin makes one dollar).

National Council of Teachers of Mathematics. *Common Core State Standards*. NCTM, 2006.

The mathematical practices presented by the National Council of Teachers of Mathematics, and found in the Common Core State Standards (NCTM, 2006), are correlated to relevant standards for understanding place value, fractions, and decimals. These practices and standards are summarized in Table 2.

Table 2: Math Practices and Decimal Relationships

Math Practice	Standards/Goals for Decimal Understanding
MP 1: Make sense of problems and persevere in solving them.	Apply understanding of operations with whole numbers and fractions to decimal concepts.
MP 2: Reason abstractly and quantitatively.	Think about/explore the fact that a number is 1/10 as much or ten times more than a number based upon left and right locations.
MP 3: Construct viable arguments and critique the reasoning of others.	Show how to represent decimals when the whole changes.
MP 6: Attend to precision.	Discuss and show how to represent 1 whole, 1 tenth, 1 hundredth, and 1 thousandth in the same model.
MP 8: Look for and express regularity in repeated reasoning.	Make a connection between the place value of whole numbers and the place value of decimal numbers.

In *Principles to Action: Ensuring Mathematical Success for All* (2004), the NCTM outlines how skills related to understanding foundational decimal concepts should progress from grade 3 to grade 6. This progression is summarized in Table 3.

National Council of Teachers of Mathematics. *Principles to Action: Ensuring Mathematical Success for All*. Reston, VA: NCTM, 2004.

Table 3: Skills Progression Leading to Understanding of Decimals

Grade 3 Skills	Grade 4 Skills	Grade 5 Skills	Grade 6 Skills
Multiplication of one-digit numbers by multiples of 10 between 10 and 90, based on place value strategies and properties of operations.	Use place value understanding to round multi-digit whole numbers to any place.	Read and write decimals to the thousandths using base ten numerals, number names, and expanded form.	Interpret and compute quotients of fractions and solve word problems using fractions by fraction multiplication and division.

National Math + Science Initiative. *Introduction to Decimals.* 2013. https://www.nms.org/Portals/0/Docs/FreeLessons/Open%20Lesson%20Grade%205%20-%20Intro%20to%20Decimals_Teacher%20and%20Student.pdf

According to the National Math + Science Initiative (2013), teachers and students generally demonstrate three common misconceptions about decimals:

1. Teachers tend to think incorrectly that decimals and fractions are two different skills, and should be taught separately.

2. Teachers tend to think incorrectly that because students know decimal place value names, they also have a conceptual understanding of decimals.

3. Students tend to misapply their knowledge of whole number place value to decimal place value, when comparing and ordering decimals. For example, they often think that 0.16 is greater than 0.2.

Martinie, Sherri L., and Jennifer M. Bay-Williams. "Investigating Students' Conceptual Understanding of Decimal Fractions Using Multiple Representations." *Mathematics Teaching in the Middle School 8*, no. 5 (January 2003): 244–247.

Ubuz, Behiye, and Betül Yayan. "Primary Teachers' Subject Matter Knowledge: Decimals." *International Journal of Mathematics Education in Science and Technology* 41, no. 6 (June 2010): 787–804.

Research shows that students and teachers alike have more difficulty understanding decimals than fractions, which has also been shown to cause struggles in math with decimals (Martinie and Bay-Williams, 2003; Ubuz and Yayan, 2010).

The methods used here approach decimal concepts through modeling with LEGO® bricks, which allow students to visualize decimals using materials that are not typical base ten materials. These methods of building, drawing, and explaining decimals allow misconceptions to come to light, since they require students to successfully visualize and prove the relationships between decimals and fractions, decimals and place value, and decimals and number operations.

HOW TO TEACH WITH THE BRICK MATH SERIES

Using the Teacher and Student Editions:
Start by taking students through the **Part 1: Show Them How** section of each chapter. Build the models, show them to the students, and ask students questions. Where directed, have students build the same models themselves so they are manipulating the bricks as you are guiding them. A document camera is helpful to display your models to the whole class as you build them. The step-by-step directions in the Teacher Edition work through several problems in Part 1. If you are using the companion Student Edition, have students draw their models and answer the questions in those books as you teach using the Teacher Edition.

Once students have mastered the modeling processes from Part 1, move to the **Part 2: Show What You Know** section of the chapter. Ask students to complete each of the problems using bricks and drawing their models. The companion Student Edition has space for writing answers and baseplate paper for drawing models. Move through the room and check that students are building their models correctly, drawing them clearly, and understanding the concepts being taught.

The Student Edition includes an assessment for each chapter, as well as additional problems for practice and challenge. The answer key for the chapter assessments can be found online on the Brick Math website, at www.brickmathseries.com/assessments. The book also includes an Assessment Chart to track each student's performance on all the skills taught in *Decimals*.

Note: Active learning breeds active learners! Students will be motivated and engaged in math when they are using bricks. It will not be silent in your classroom, but it will be full of chatter about the math!

Suggested Bricks:
Brick Math is designed to be used with LEGO® bricks or LEGO®-compatible bricks. If you already have bricks, your students should be able to use them to make the models. They may have to combine smaller bricks together when the directions call for longer bricks such as 1x10s or 2x12s. Each student also needs a baseplate on which to build brick models.

Each chapter lists the bricks suggested for the lessons in that chapter, and the appendix includes a total brick inventory of all the bricks suggested for the program, which can be shared by two students.

Specially designed Brick Math brick sets are available for purchase from Brigantine Media. Brick sets are packaged in divided boxes and include a baseplate for each student.

Classroom Management Ideas:
- Before starting, have a conversation with the students about using bricks as a learning tool rather than a toy.
- Teach students the language of bricks (baseplate, stud, 1x1, 1x2, etc.).
- Assign brick sets to specific students and always give the same students the same sets. An easy way to do this is to number each brick set and assign the sets to pairs of students by number. When students know that they will always have to work with the same brick set, they are more likely to be careful that the bricks are returned to the set.
- Do not teach using bricks—or any manipulative—every day. Students also need to have opportunities to think through the math processes without having a physical object for modeling. Sometimes it helps to have students draw models without building them with bricks first. Remember, they won't have access to manipulatives during most tests when they have to show what they have learned.

- To keep bricks clean, put the bricks in a hosiery bag and wash them on the top rack of the dishwasher. Let them air dry. Clean bricks before assigning sets to new students.
- To keep bricks from sliding off desks, use foam shelf liner cut into rectangular pieces, or large meat trays (you can often get these free from a local supermarket).
- Inventory the sets twice a year and replace bricks as needed. There are a variety of vendors online that sell specific bricks, both new and used. LEGO® retail stores also sell a variety of individual bricks.

INTRODUCING DECIMALS

Students will learn/discover:
- The definition of a decimal
- How to model decimals using bricks in a decimal grid
- How to model the place values of decimals
- How to write decimals in expanded form
- The similarities between whole number place values and decimal place values
- How to identify decimal numbers as fractions of 100

Why is this important?
Understanding how to read and write decimals is an important skill used in counting money, measuring distance, and statistical analysis. Understanding decimal place value is necessary for reading and writing decimals and using them in real-world situations. In order to grasp how decimal place values work, students must first have a firm foundation in whole number place value.

Vocabulary:
- **Decimal number:** A number with a fractional part represented by figures to the right of a decimal point; these figures are the numerator of the equivalent fraction, whose denominator is a power of ten (e.g., the decimal .2 is equivalent to $2/10$ or $20/100$)
- **Mixed decimal:** A number that includes a whole and a fractional part; the whole number is represented by figures to the left of the decimal point, while the fractional part is represented by figures to the right of the decimal point (e.g., 1.25)

SUGGESTED BRICKS

Size	Number
1x1	24
1x2	25
1x3	12
1x4	10
1x6	4
1x8	4
1x10	2
1x12	2
2x2	6
2x3	6
2x4	6

Note: Using a baseplate helps keep the bricks in place. One baseplate is suggested for these activities.

- **Decimal notation:** A representation of a fraction or other real number using the base ten system, with any of the digits 0, 1, 2, 3, 4, 5, 6, 7, 8, 9, and a decimal point
- **Tenth:** One of 10 equal parts of a whole (10^{-1} or $1/10$ or .10); in decimal notation, the tenths place is the first place value position to the right of the decimal point
- **Hundredth:** One of 100 equal parts of a whole (10^{-2} or $1/100$ or .01); in decimal notation, the hundredths place is the second place value position to the right of the decimal point
- **Thousandth:** One of 1000 equal parts of a whole (10^{-3} or $1/1000$ or .001); in decimal notation, the thousandths place is the third place value position to the right of the decimal point
- **Expanded form:** A math sentence for a decimal number that shows all place value positions within the number (e.g., 1.25 = 1 + .20 + .05)

How to use the companion student book, *Decimals Using LEGO® Bricks–Student Edition*:
- After students build their models, have them draw the models and explain their thinking in the Student Edition. Recording the models on paper after building them with bricks helps reinforce the concepts being taught.
- Discuss the vocabulary for each lesson with students as they work through the Student Edition.
- Use the chapter assessments in the Student Edition to gauge student understanding of the content.

Part 1: Show Them How

Ask students to define a decimal and what it represents (*answer:* like a fraction, a decimal is a form of notation used to represent a part of a whole). *Note:* It is important that students make the connection between decimal and fractional representations of parts of a whole.

Explain to students that they will be learning two ways to model decimal numbers using bricks: the place value model and the decimal grid model.

The Place Value Model:

Remind students how to model decimal place value using bricks. *Note*: See *Basic Measurement Using LEGO Bricks—Teacher Edition* (Chapter 6) to review decimal place value models.

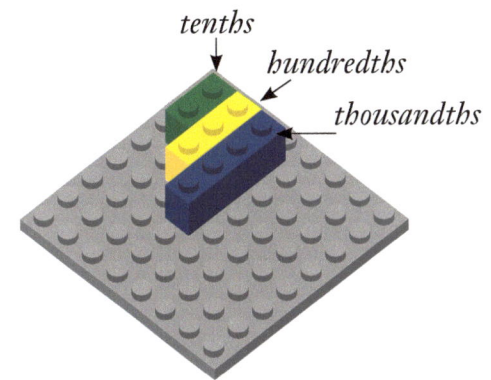

Place value model:
1x2 brick = tenths place = $1/10$ = 0.1
1x3 brick = hundredths place = $1/100$ = 0.01
1x4 brick = thousandths place = $1/1000$ = 0.001

Note: Students should use a 1x1 brick to represent the decimal point. It is helpful to use the same brick color to represent the decimal point every time, especially when building mixed decimals (which also use 1x1 bricks to represent the place value for ones).

Discuss the relationship between a fractional part and a decimal part. *Note:* It is helpful for students to think about money as an example (e.g., fifty cents as a fractional part is $1/2$ of a dollar, while the same amount as a decimal part is 0.50 of a dollar).

Problem #1: Model this decimal: 0.23

1. Ask students to identify the bricks needed to show the tenths (*answer:* two 1x2 bricks) and the hundredths (*answer:* three 1x3 bricks).

2. Build a place value model for the decimal 0.23 using those bricks. Have students draw the model and label the place values in the decimal.

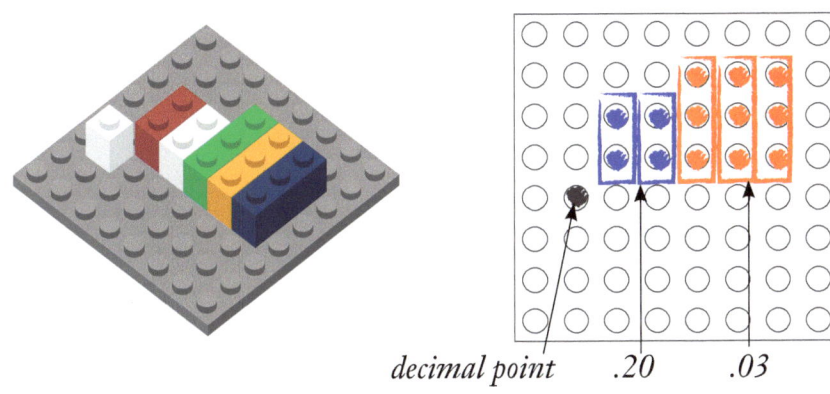

decimal point   .20   .03

DR. SHIRLEY DISSELER | DECIMALS USING LEGO® BRICKS—TEACHER EDITION

3. Show students how to write the math sentence for the decimal in expanded form (*answer*: 0.20 + 0.03 = 0.23).

Problem #2: Model this decimal: 2.31

1. Have students identify what type of decimal 2.31 is (*answer*: a mixed decimal). Discuss the definition of a mixed decimal and its similarity to a mixed fraction.

2. Ask students to identify the bricks needed to model the decimal (*answer*: two 1x1 bricks for the whole number, three 1x2 bricks for the tenths, and one 1x3 brick for the hundredths).

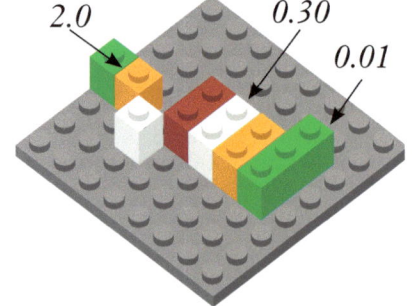

3. Show students how to use bricks to build a place value model for the decimal. *Note:* Model the decimal point with a 1x1 brick one row below the model of the decimal, so the brick that models the decimal point is clearly understood.

4. Have students draw the model and label the place values in the decimal. Have students write a math sentence for the decimal in expanded form (*answer*: 2.0 + 0.30 + 0.01 = 2.31).

Problem #3: Have students model this decimal: 2.453

1. Ask students to select the bricks needed to build a place value model for 2.453. Have students discuss their selections with a partner, and then build the model.

2. Have students draw the model, and write a math sentence for the decimal in expanded form (*answer*: 2.0 + 0.4 + 0.05 + 0.003 = 2.453).

3. Ask students to discuss how decimal place values are similar to whole number place values (*answer*: in both cases, moving between place values requires multiplication or division by 10).

Decimal Grid Model:
Explain to students that you are going to build a Brick Math decimal grid, a 10 x 10 grid with 100 studs inside, which is used to model decimal numbers.

1. Build a rectangle on a baseplate using two 1x10 bricks and two 1x12 bricks. Place the 1x12 bricks horizontally on the top and bottom of the model, and place the 1x10 bricks vertically on each side. Have students build the same model along with you.

2. Ask students to count the number of studs *inside* the rectangle (*answer:* 100 studs). Explain that this is a decimal grid. Have students identify the shape of the grid (*answer:* the grid is a 10 x 10 square). *Note:* Make sure students do not count the sides of the grid (i.e., the 1x10 and 1x12 bricks), because those bricks are not inside the square.

3. Explain that each stud inside the grid represents one hundredth, and each 1x10 column or row of studs represents one tenth, because it contains 10 of the 100 studs.

4. Show students how to model a decimal number. As an example, model 0.25 by covering 25 studs with a combination of bricks. *Note:* If possible, use bricks that are all the same color to represent the decimal number inside the decimal grid.

5. Ask students to model 0.30 in a decimal grid using three 1x10 bricks. *Note:* Remind students not to count the sides of the model.

   Point out that each 1x10 brick has 10 studs, so they willl cover 30 of the 100 total studs in the grid.

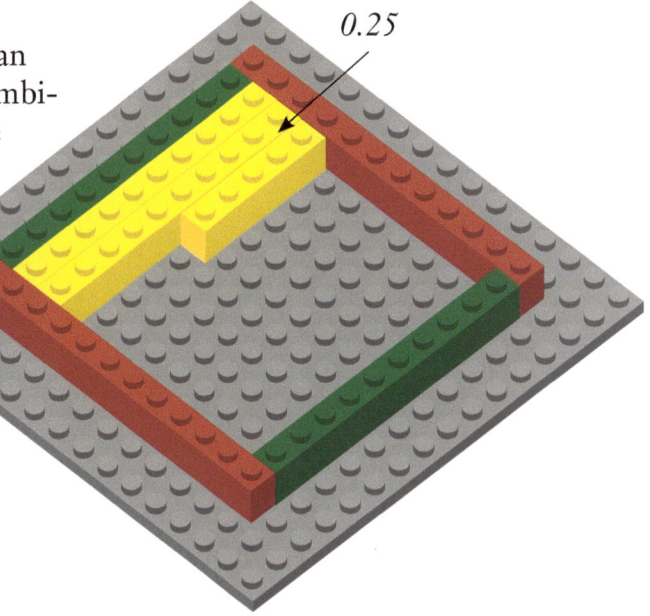

0.30

Ask students how to express this as a fractional part of the whole grid (*answer:* $30/100$). Ask students how many tenths are shown in the model (*answer:* 3 tenths). Ask students how 3 tenths are written as a fraction (*answer:* $3/10$). *Note:* Make sure students understand that decimals are another way to write a fractional part of a number.

6. Have students build 0.6 using the grid model. Have them draw their model and explain their thinking, then write a fraction for the decimal. To get students started with the process of modeling, ask how many 1x10 bricks (or sets of 10 studs) are needed to show 6 tenths in the decimal grid (*answer:* six 1x10 bricks). *Note:* If students do not have six 1x10 bricks, use a combination of smaller bricks to cover 60 studs.

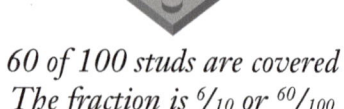

60 of 100 studs are covered
The fraction is $6/10$ or $60/100$

Part 2: Show What You Know

1. Can you use a decimal grid model to show 0.23? Draw and label the model. Write a fraction for the decimal.

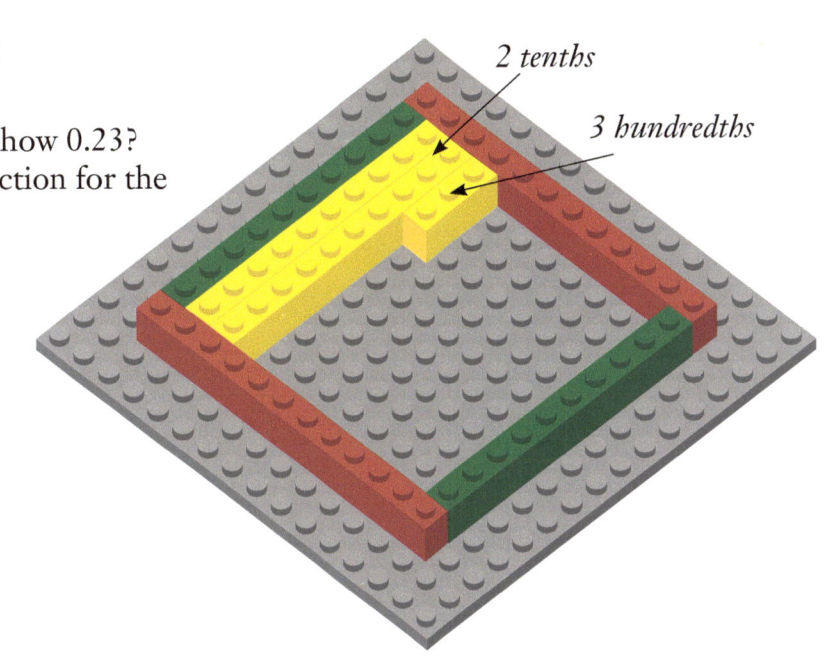

Solution:

23 of 100 studs are covered
The fraction is $^{23}/_{100}$

2. Can you use a decimal grid model to show 0.5? Draw and label the model. Write two fractions for the decimal.

Solution:

5 tenths or 50 hundredths
$^{5}/_{10}$ or $^{50}/_{100}$

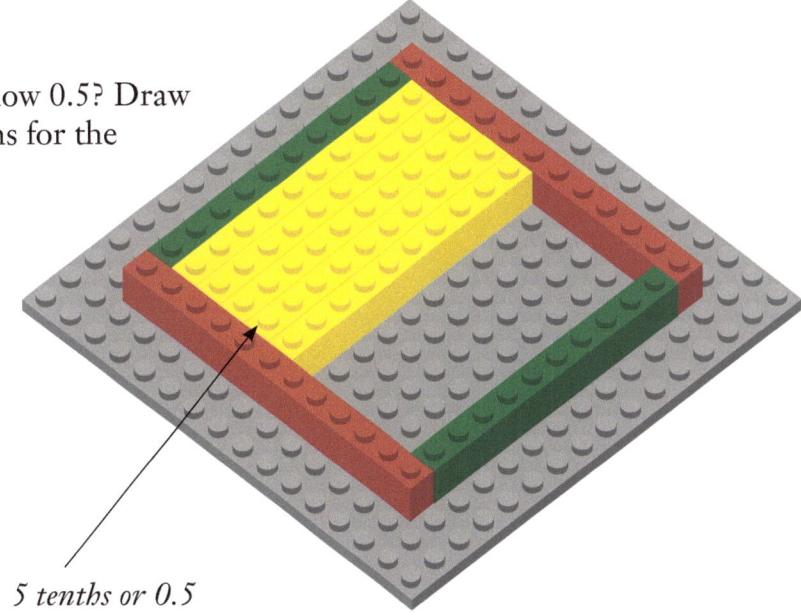

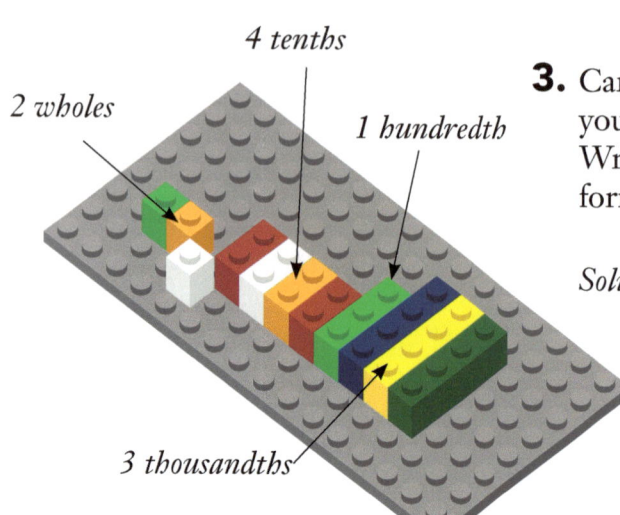

3. Can you use a place value model to show 2.413? Draw your model and label the parts of the decimal number. Write a math sentence for the decimal in expanded form.

Solution: 2.0 + 0.4 + 0.01 + 0.003 = 2.413

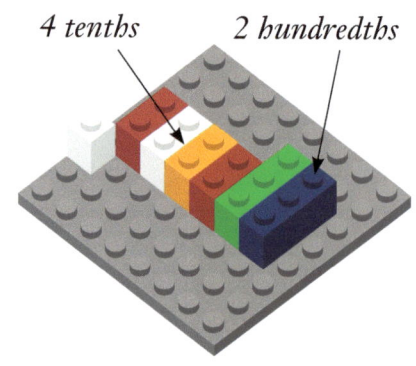

4. Can you use a place value model to show 0.42? Draw your model and label the parts of the decimal number. Write a math sentence for the decimal in expanded form.

Solution: 0.4 + 0.02 = 0.42

5. Partner build: Using either a place value model or a decimal grid model, build a decimal number without allowing your partner to see it. Exchange models. Identify the decimal number and the place values in your partner's model. Draw and label the place values in your partner's decimal, and write a math sentence for the decimal in expanded form.

Solutions will vary.

ORDERING DECIMALS

SUGGESTED BRICKS

Size	Number
1x1	24
1x2	25
1x3	12

Note: Using a baseplate helps keep the bricks in place. One baseplate is suggested for these activities.

Students will learn/discover:
- The value of decimal numbers
- How to show decimals in order of value
- How to determine whether the value of one decimal is greater or less than the value of another

Why is this important?
Before students learn about decimals, they learn how to compare whole numbers to determine if the value of one number is greater than or less than the value of another. But students often do not realize that decimal numbers can be compared the same way. An understanding of how to compare decimal number values is necessary for many real-life skills and activities, including comparisons of monetary values and event times. Seeing decimals as numbers that can be compared is a key skill in creating fluency with the number system.

Vocabulary:
- **Decimal number:** A number with a fractional part represented by figures to the right of a decimal point; these figures are the numerator of the equivalent fraction, whose denominator is a power of ten (e.g., the decimal .2 is equivalent to $^2/_{10}$ or $^{20}/_{100}$)
- **Decimal notation:** A representation of a fraction or other real number using the base ten system, with any of the digits 0, 1, 2, 3, 4, 5, 6, 7, 8, 9, and a decimal point
- **Tenth:** One of 10 equal parts of a whole (10^{-1} or $1/_{10}$ or .10); in decimal notation, the tenths place is the first place value position to the right of the decimal point

- **Hundredth:** One of 100 equal parts of a whole (10^{-2} or $1/100$ or .01); in decimal notation, the hundredths place is the second place value position to the right of the decimal point
- **Thousandth:** One of 1000 equal parts of a whole (10^{-3} or $1/1000$ or .001); in decimal notation, the thousandths place is the third place value position to the right of the decimal point
- **Expanded form:** A math sentence for a decimal number that shows all place value positions within the number (e.g., 1.25 = 1 + .20 + .05)
- **Greater than symbol (>):** Inserted between two numbers to indicate that the number on the left is larger than the number on the right
- **Less than symbol (<):** Inserted between two numbers to indicate that the number on the left is smaller than the number on the right

How to use the companion student book, *Decimals Using LEGO® Bricks–Student Edition*:
- After students build their models, have them draw the models and explain their thinking in the Student Edition. Recording the models on paper after building them with bricks helps reinforce the concepts being taught.
- Discuss the vocabulary for each lesson with students as they work through the Student Edition.
- Use the chapter assessments in the Student Edition to gauge student understanding of the content.

Part 1: Show Them How

Review the decimal place value modeling method (Chapter 1).

Ask students to explain the meaning of the following math symbols:

>	Greater than
<	Less than
≥	Greater than or equal to
≤	Less than or equal to

Explain to students that in these lessons, they will learn to compare decimal numbers and mixed decimals.

Problem #1: Compare these decimals: 0.34 and 0.44

1. Have students build a place value model of 0.34. Have students build 0.44 below the first model, and write the expanded form for each decimal.

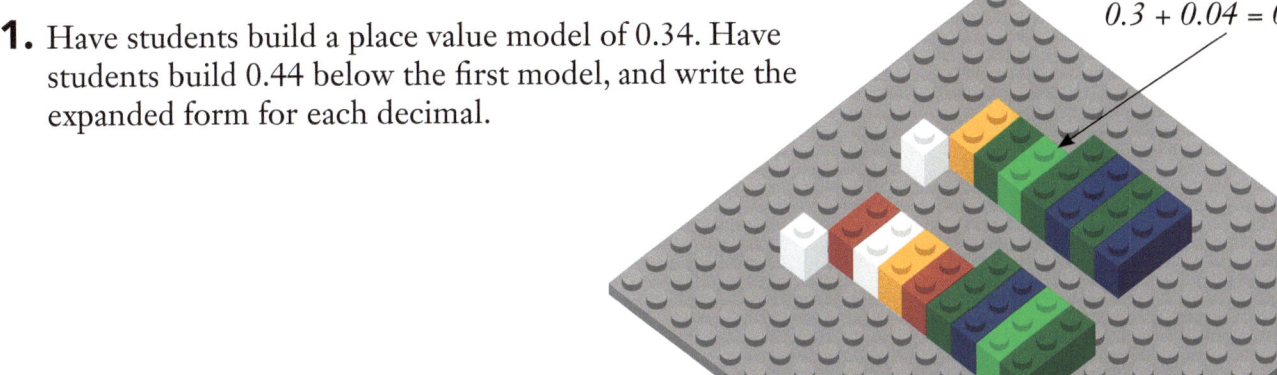

0.3 + 0.04 = 0.34

0.4 + 0.04 = 0.44

2. Ask students what they notice when they compare the two decimals (*answer:* 0.44 has one more tenth in the tenths place than 0.34). Ask students what this means (*answer:* 0.44 is a larger number than 0.34). *Note:* It can be helpful to encourage students to think of each decimal in terms of money, in which case 34 cents is less money than 44 cents.

3. Show students how to write the math sentence to compare these two numbers (*answer:* 0.34 < 0.44). *Note:* The order of the decimals in the math sentence should mirror the order of the decimals in the original problem (0.34 < 0.44, not 0.44 > 0.34).

Problem #2: Compare these decimals: 0.25 and 0.50

1. Build place value models of the two decimal numbers.

2. Ask students to compare the two decimals (*possible answers:* 0.25 has 2 tenths and 0.50 has 5 tenths; 0.50 has no hundredths and 0.25 has 5 hundredths).

3. Show students how to determine which decimal is larger by comparing the largest place value for each one to see

which has the most bricks. Ask students which of the two decimals is larger (*answer:* 0.50 is the larger decimal, since it has more bricks in the tenths place).

4. Have students write a math sentence to compare these two decimals (*answer:* 0.25 < 0.50).

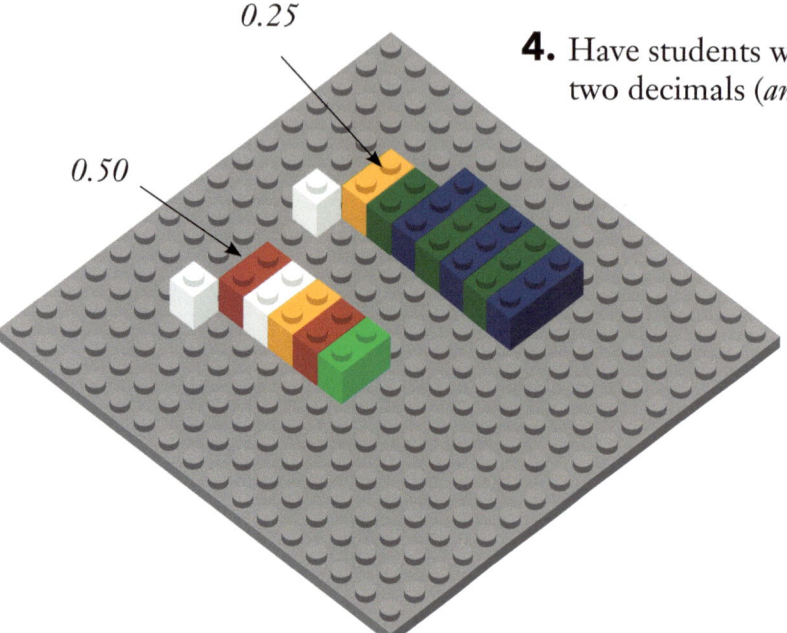

0.25

0.50

Problem #3: Compare these decimals: 0.31 and 0.35

1. Have students build place value models of 0.31 and 0.35.

2. Ask students what they notice when they compare the tenths place of both models (*answer:* they have the same number of bricks).

3. Ask students how to determine which decimal is larger (*answer:* compare the number of bricks in the hundredths place of each model).

0.31

0.35

4. Ask students to count the number of bricks in the hundredths place of each model, and identify which of the two decimals is larger (*answer:* 0.35 is larger, because it has five bricks in the hundredths place, while 0.31 has one brick in the hundredths place). Have students write a math sentence to compare these two decimals (*answer:* 0.31 < 0.35).

Problem #4: Compare these decimals: 1.2, 1.23, and 1.32

1. Have students build place value models of the three decimal numbers.

2. Ask students how to determine the order of these three decimals from least to greatest (*answer:* start by comparing the largest place value in the decimals). Compare the whole number values of the three decimals (*answer:* all three whole numbers have a value of 1).

   Since the whole number values are the same, compare the tenths place values of the three decimals (*answer:* the first two models both have 2 tenths, but the third model has 3 tenths, so 1.32 is the largest decimal).

   Compare the hundredths place values of 1.2 and 1.23 to determine which is larger (*answer:* since 1.23 has 3 in the hundredths place and 1.2 has no digit in the hundredths place, 1.23 is larger).

3. Have students write the decimals from least to greatest with a math sentence that uses proper notation (*answer:* 1.2 < 1.23 < 1.32). Have students draw their models and explain their thinking.

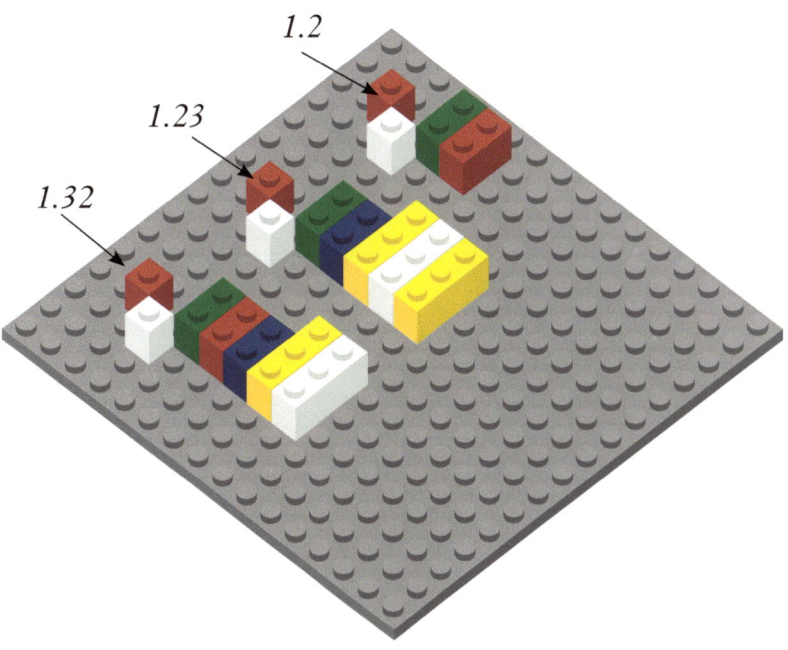

Part 2: Show What You Know

1. Can you build place value models of 0.45 and 0.43? Draw and label your models. Circle the drawing of the larger decimal and explain why it is larger. Write a math sentence using the "greater than" symbol.

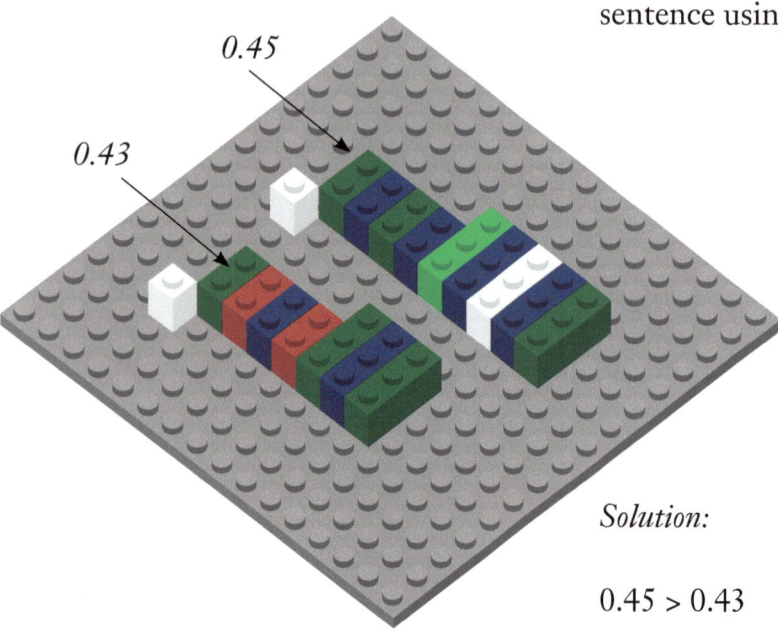

Solution:

0.45 > 0.43

The two decimals have the same number of bricks in the tenths place, but 0.45 has more 1x3 bricks in the hundredths place than 0.43.

2. Can you build place value models of 2.31 and 1.13? Draw and label your models. Circle the drawing of the smaller decimal and explain why it is smaller. Write a math sentence using the "less than" symbol.

Solution:

1.13 < 2.31 because 2.31 has a larger whole number value than 1.13.

3. Can you build place value models of 2.12, 2.3, and 1.33? Draw and label your models. Write a math sentence by placing the decimals in order from least to greatest, using "less than" symbols. Explain your thinking.

Solution:

1.33 < 2.12 < 2.3

1.33 is the smallest decimal because it has the smallest whole number value; 2.3 is the largest because it has a larger tenths place value than 2.12.

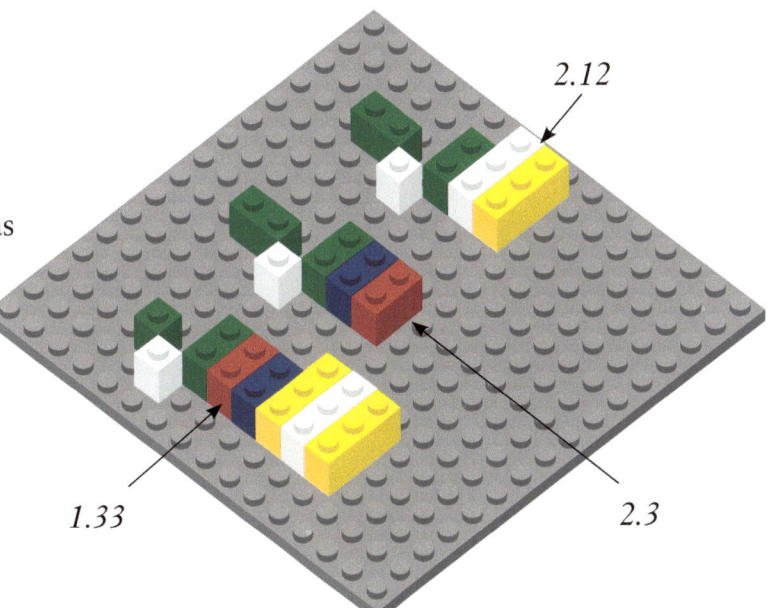

3

SUGGESTED BRICKS

Size	Number
1x1	30
1x2	25
1x3	12
1x4	10
1x10	2
1x12	2
2x2	10
2x3	6
2x4	4

Note: Using a baseplate helps keep the bricks in place. One baseplate is suggested for these activities.

FRACTION EQUIVALENTS OF DECIMALS

Students will learn/discover:
- How to model decimal numbers using a 10 x 10 decimal grid
- How to identify decimal numbers as fractions of 100

Why is this important?
Understanding how to read and write decimals up to one whole is an important skill that will help students develop an understanding of fractional and monetary equivalents. Learning how to identify decimal numbers based on hundredths will help students connect decimals with fractions. The deciaml grid model used in this chapter helps students visualize this connection: one stud in the grid is equal to one hundredth of a whole, and 10 studs is equal to one tenth of a whole. The decimal grid model also helps students visualize monetary amounts, relating pennies to dimes and dimes to one dollar (e.g., one stud equals one penny, or one hundredth of a dollar).

Vocabulary:
- **Decimal number:** A number with a fractional part represented by figures to the right of a decimal point; these figures are the numerator of the equivalent fraction, whose denominator is a power of ten (e.g., the decimal .2 is equivalent to $^2/_{10}$ or $^{20}/_{100}$)
- **Decimal notation:** A representation of a fraction or other real number using the base ten system, with any of the digits 0, 1, 2, 3, 4, 5, 6, 7, 8, 9, and a decimal point

- **Tenth:** One of 10 equal parts of a whole (10^{-1} or $1/10$ or .10); in decimal notation, the tenths place is the first place value position to the right of the decimal point
- **Hundredth:** One of 100 equal parts of a whole (10^{-2} or $1/100$ or .01); in decimal notation, the hundredths place is the second place value position to the right of the decimal point

How to use the companion student book, *Decimals Using LEGO® Bricks–Student Edition*:
- After students build their models, have them draw the models and explain their thinking in the Student Edition. Recording the models on paper after building them with bricks helps reinforce the concepts being taught.
- Discuss the vocabulary for each lesson with students as they work through the Student Edition.
- Use the chapter assessments in the Student Edition to gauge student understanding of the content.

Part 1: Show Them How

Review the definition of a decimal and what it represents (*answer:* like a fraction, a decimal is a form of notation used to represent a part of a whole). *Note:* It is important that students make the connection between decimal and fractional representations of parts of a whole.

Review how to build a decimal grid (Chapter 1):

Step 1: Have students build a rectangle on a baseplate using two 1x10 bricks and two 1x12 bricks. *Note:* the 1x12 bricks should be placed horizontally on the top and bottom of the model, and the 1x10 bricks should be placed vertically on each side.

Step 2: Ask students to count the number of studs *inside* the rectangle (*answer:* 100 studs). Explain that this is a decimal grid. Have students identify the shape of the grid (*answer:* the grid is a 10 x 10 square). *Note:* Remind students not to count the sides of the grid (i.e., the 1x10 and 1x12 bricks), because those bricks are not inside the square.

Step 3: Explain that each stud inside the grid represents one hundredth, and each 1x10 column or row of studs represents one tenth, because it contains 10 of the 100 studs.

Problem #1: Model 0.25 + 0.50 using a decimal grid

1. Build a model of 0.25 in the decimal grid by covering 25 studs with a combination of bricks that are all the same color. Have students build the same model. Have students name the fractional representation of 0.25 (answer: ¼ or ²⁵⁄₁₀₀). *Note*: It may be helpful for students to think in monetary terms (i.e., 25 cents as what fraction of one dollar).

2. Add 0.50 to the model using bricks that are a different color. Have students add 0.50 to their models.

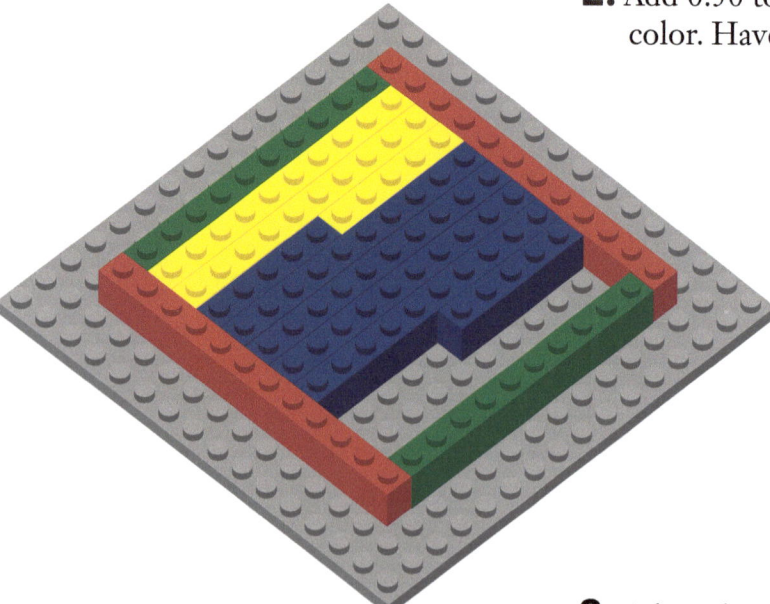

3. Ask students what they notice about the two decimal amounts (*answer*: 0.50 has twice the number of studs as 0.25).

4. Ask students how many studs in the decimal grid are covered (*answer:* 75 studs). Have them record the decimal and the fraction for that amount (*answer:* 0.75 and $^{75}/_{100}$). Make sure students understand that the fraction is $^{75}/_{100}$ because 75 of 100 studs are covered.

Problem #2: Model .01 of the whole using a decimal grid

1. Ask students which brick can represent .01 (*answer:* one 1x1 brick). Discuss why only one 1x1 brick is used for this model (*answer:* the grid has 100 studs, each representing one hundredth of the whole; one 1x1 brick is equivalent to 0.01 of the whole).

2. Ask students to identify the fractional equivalent of 0.01 (*answer:* $^{1}/_{100}$). Make sure that students understand that the fraction is $^{1}/_{100}$ because 1 of 100 studs is covered.

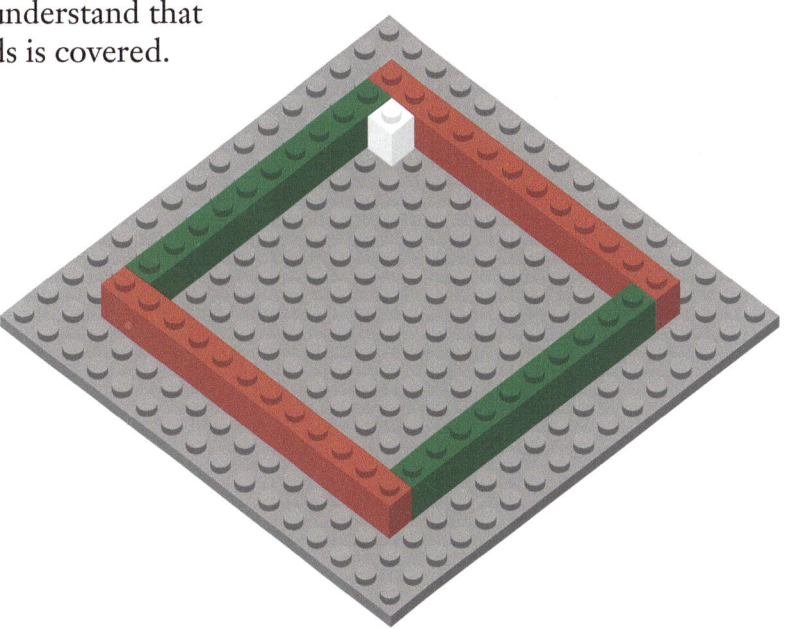

Problem #3: Model 0.10 of the whole using a decimal grid

1. Ask students which brick can represent 0.10 (*answer:* one 1x10 brick). Discuss what they notice when they place the 1x10 brick in the decimal grid (*answer:* 10 of 100 studs are covered).

2. Show students how to write 0.10 as two different fractional amounts (*answer:* $1/10$ or $10/100$). *Note:* Students should notice that when one zero is added to the numerator of the fraction, one zero is also added to the denominator.

   Make sure students understand that the amount covered is 10 of 100 studs, which is 0.10. This decimal can be written as the fraction $1/10$ or $10/100$.

Part 2: Show What You Know

1. Can you build a model that shows 0.42, using a decimal grid? Draw and explain your model, and write the fraction equivalent.

   Solution:

   42 out of 100 studs are covered, so the fraction is $42/100$

2. Can you build a model of two decimals that together show 0.30, using a decimal grid? Draw and explain your model and label the two decimals. Write the fraction equivalent for each decimal. *Note:* Students do not need to simplify the fractions.

Possible solution:

Decimals used: 0.16 and 0.14
Fraction equivalents: $^{16}/_{100}$ and $^{14}/_{100}$

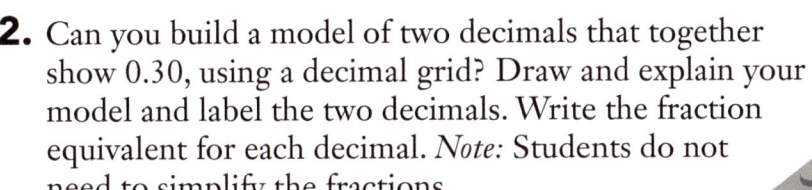

3. Can you build a model that shows 0.20, using a decimal grid? Draw and explain your model. Write two fraction equivalents for the decimal.

Solution:

Fraction equivalents: $^{2}/_{10}$ and $^{20}/_{100}$

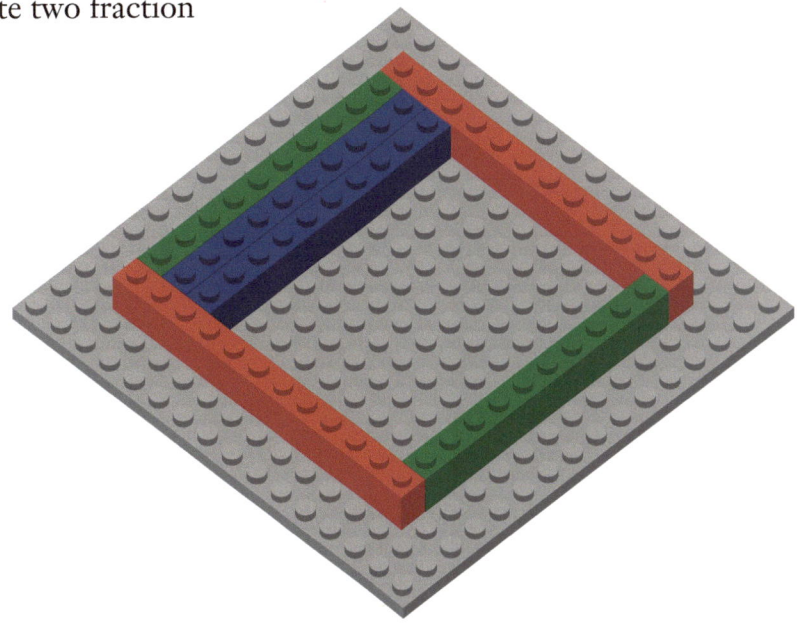

4

SUGGESTED BRICKS

Size	Number
1x1	24
1x2	25
1x3	12
1x4	10
1x6	4
1x8	4
1x10	2
1x12	2
2x2	6
2x3	6
2x4	6

Note: Using a baseplate helps keep the bricks in place. One baseplate is suggested for these activities.

DECIMALS AS MONEY AND TIME

Students will learn/discover:
- How to relate decimal notation to monetary amounts
- How to read a decimal as money
- How to use decimals in comparing measurements of time

Why is this important?
Real-life applications are key to helping students see the "why" behind learning about decimals. Money and time are two excellent life skills for straightforward application of the knowledge of decimals. Understanding decimals is also very important to scientific fields.

Vocabulary:
- **Decimal number:** A number with a fractional part, represented by figures to the right of a decimal point; these figures are the numerator of the equivalent fraction, whose denominator is a power of ten (e.g., the decimal .2 is equivalent to $^2/_{10}$ or $^{20}/_{100}$)
- **Decimal notation:** A representation of a fraction or other real number using the base ten system, with any of the digits 0, 1, 2, 3, 4, 5, 6, 7, 8, 9, and a decimal point
- **Tenth:** One of 10 equal parts of a whole (10^{-1} or $^1/_{10}$ or .10); in decimal notation, the tenths place is the first place value position to the right of the decimal point
- **Hundredth:** One of 100 equal parts of a whole (10^{-2} or $^1/_{100}$ or .01); in decimal notation, the hundredths place is the second place value position to the right of the decimal point

- **Thousandth:** One of 1000 equal parts of a whole (10^{-3} or $1/1000$ or .001); in decimal notation, the thousandths place is the third place value position to the right of the decimal point
- **Expanded form:** A math sentence for a decimal number that shows all place value positions within the number (e.g. 1.25 = 1 + .20 + .05)

How to use the companion student book, *Decimals Using LEGO® Bricks–Student Edition*:
- After students build their models, have them draw the models and explain their thinking in the Student Edition. Recording the models on paper after building them with bricks helps reinforce the concepts being taught.
- Discuss the vocabulary for each lesson with students as they work through the Student Edition.
- Use the chapter assessments in the Student Edition to gauge student understanding of the content.

Part 1: Show Them How

Review the definition of a decimal and what it represents (*answer:* like a fraction, a decimal is a form of notation used to represent a part of a whole). *Note:* It is important that students make the connection between decimal and fractional representations of parts of a whole.

Review how to model place value of fractional amounts using bricks. *Note:* See *Basic Measurement Using LEGO® Bricks—Teacher Edition* to review place value models.

Place Value Model:
1x2 brick = tenths place = $1/10$ = 0.1
1x3 brick = hundredths place = $1/100$ = 0.01
1x4 brick = thousandths place = $1/1000$ = 0.001
Note: Use a 1x1 brick to represent the decimal point. It is helpful to use the same brick color to represent the decimal point every time, especially when building mixed decimals (which also use 1x1 bricks to represent the place value for ones).

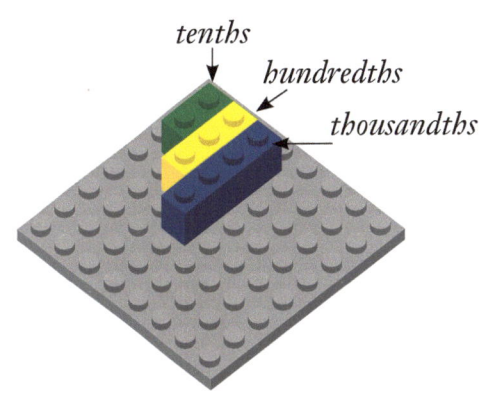

Review the decimal grid model for representing decimal numbers introduced in chapter 1.

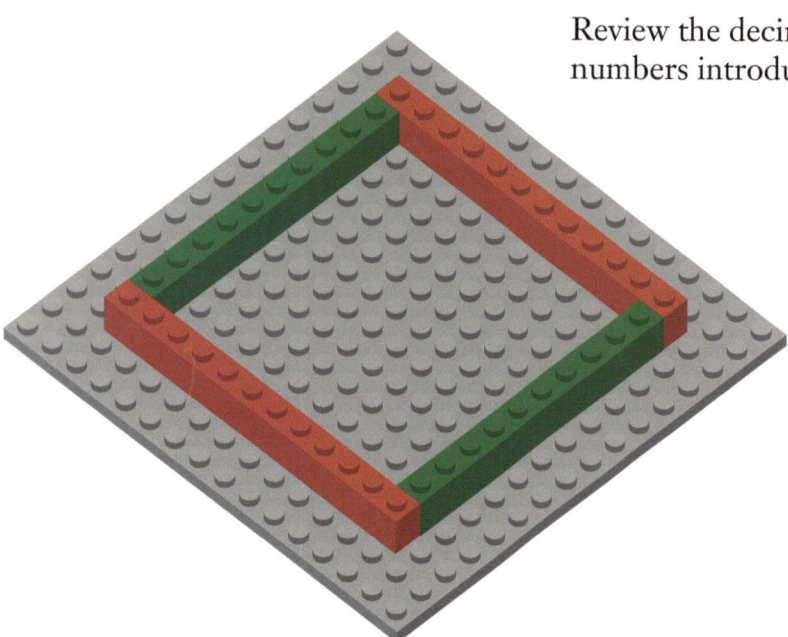

100 studs inside decimal grid

Problem #1: John ran one half-mile in 4.23 minutes. Build a decimal place value model to show the amount of time that John took to complete his run.

Explain to students that 4.23 minutes means 4 minutes and 23 hundredths of another minute. Build a model that shows the number 4.23. Have students draw and describe this model. *Note:* Since this decimal includes a whole number, students should represent it using the place value model, not the grid model.

4.23

Problem #2: Shane also ran the race and finished in 4 minutes and 31 hundredths of another minute. Build a model for the amount of time that Shane's run took, and add the model to the same baseplate, directly under the model for John's run.

Ask students who ran the race faster, and by how much (*answer:* John ran it faster, by 8 hundredths of a minute). Have them explain their thinking (*answer:* a comparison of the two decimal models shows that John's decimal is .08 smaller than Shane's).

John's run

Shane's run

Problem #3: In the high school swim competition, Mia, Lisa, and Chris had the following finish times for the 50-meter freestyle:

Mia	.35 minutes
Lisa	.41 minutes
Chris	.32 minutes

Build a model for each swimmer's decimal time and compare them. Who came in first, second, and third? How do you know from looking at the model?

(*answer:* first = Chris; second = Mia; third = Lisa; the smallest decimal is the fastest time).

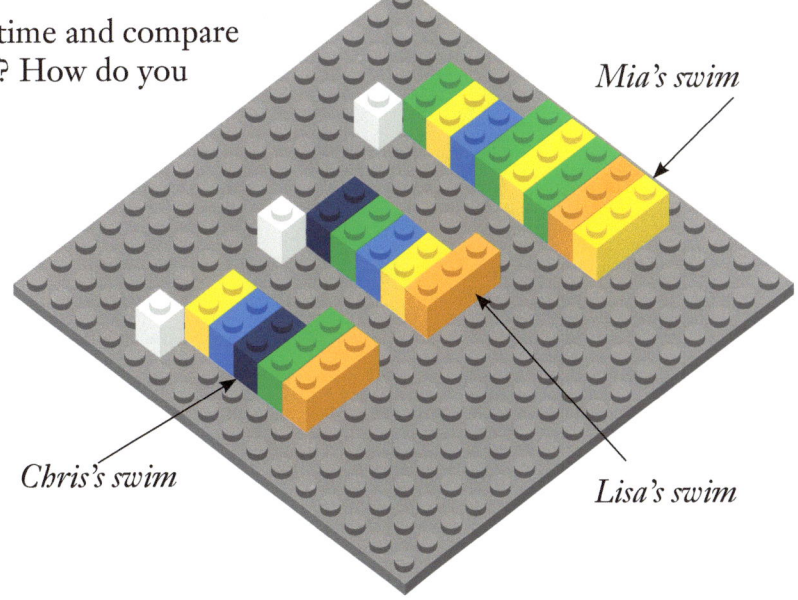

Mia's swim

Chris's swim

Lisa's swim

Problem #4: Sophie has 25 cents (0.25) and Angie has 22 cents (0.22). How much money do they have altogether?

Note: Students can use either the place value model or the decimal grid model to approach this problem. For students who struggle to understand place value, the decimal grid model may be the best approach.

Place value model:

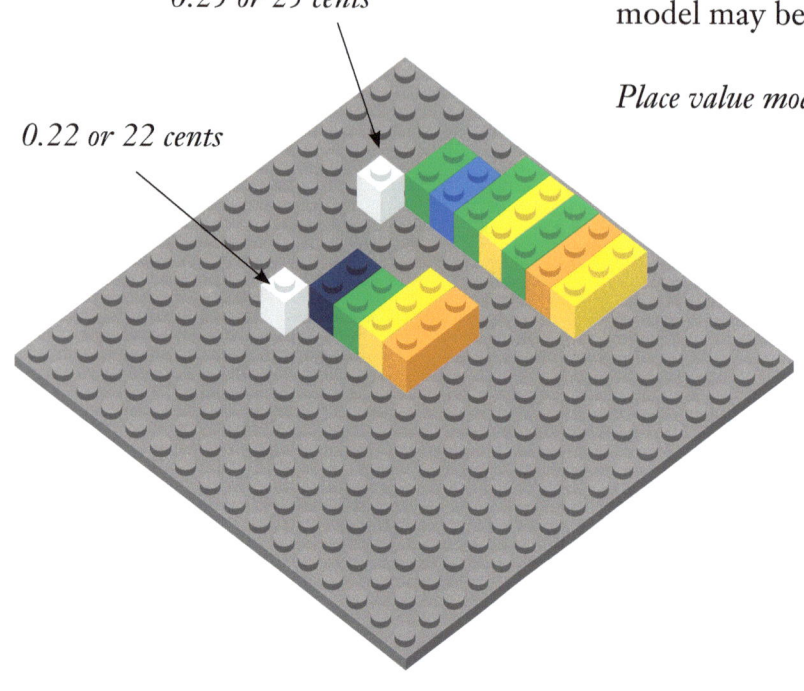

0.25 or 25 cents

0.22 or 22 cents

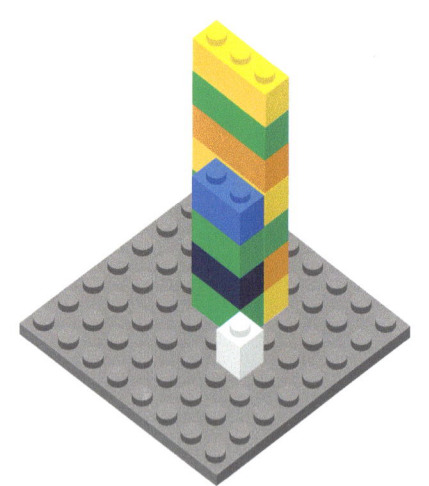

To model the amount of money that Sophie and Angie have together, stack the same-sized bricks from both models.

Count the number of each size brick, and add the amounts together (*answer:* Sophie and Angie have 4 tenths [four 1x2 bricks] and 7 hundredths [seven 1x3 bricks], or 0.47 [47 cents]).

Decimal grid model:

Count the number of studs in the grid that are covered by bricks (*answer*: 47 studs covered, showing 0.47 or 47 cents altogether).

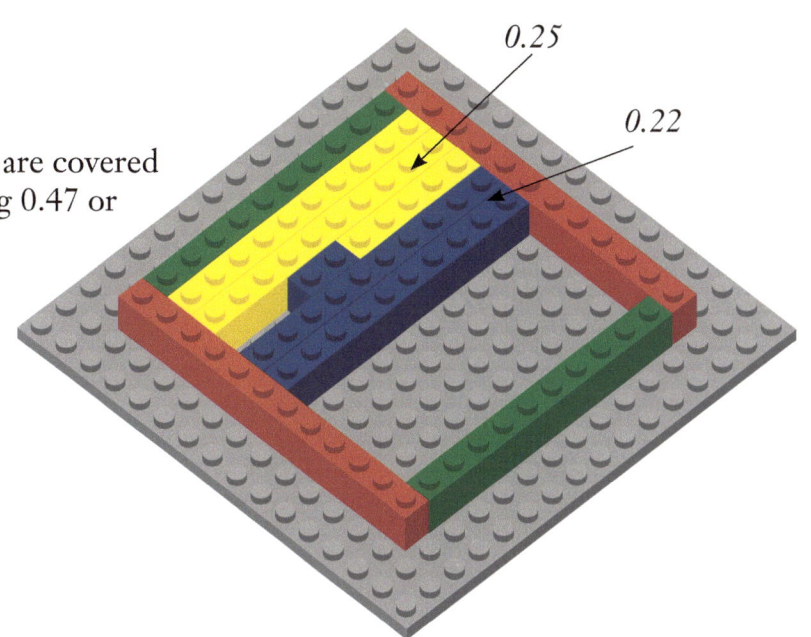

Part 2: Show What You Know

1. The track teams ran a race and posted these times for the 50-yard dash:

Team 1: 8.2 seconds
Team 2: 9.1 seconds
Team 3: 8.21 seconds

Build models of the three teams' times. Draw the models and explain how you know which team came in first, second, and third place.

Solution:

Team 1 finished in first place, Team 3 finished in second place, and Team 2 finished in third place.

Both Team 1 and Team 3 have a smaller whole number value (8, shown by eight 1x1 bricks) than Team 2 (9, shown by nine 1x1 bricks); Team 1 has a smaller hundredths value (0, shown by zero 1x3 bricks) than Team 3 (1, shown by one 1x3 brick).

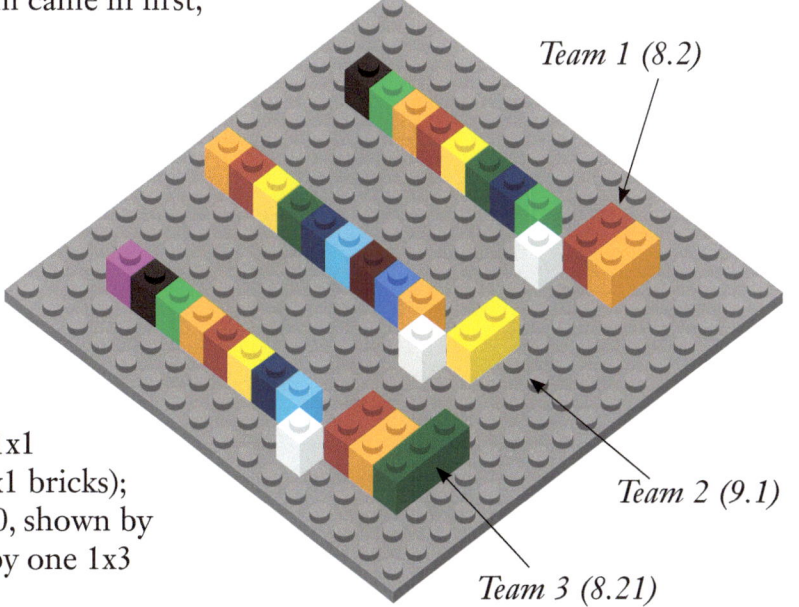

DR. SHIRLEY DISSELER | DECIMALS USING LEGO® BRICKS—TEACHER EDITION

2. If three students have enough coins between them to make a dollar, what possible combinations of coins could they have? Build a decimal grid model showing 3 decimal amounts that are equivalent to a dollar when combined. Draw and label the decimals in your model, and explain your thinking.

Note: There are many solutions to this problem.

Possible solution:

0.25 + 0.25 + 0.50 = 1.00
100 studs are covered, equivalent to 1.00

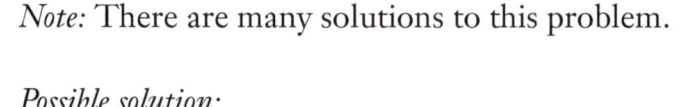

3. A soda costs $1.25 and a slice of pizza costs $2.50. How much money is needed to purchase both? Build a model to show each decimal amount. Draw and label your models. Stack the same-sized bricks from both models together to show the total decimal amount.

Solution:
$1.25 + $2.50 = $3.75

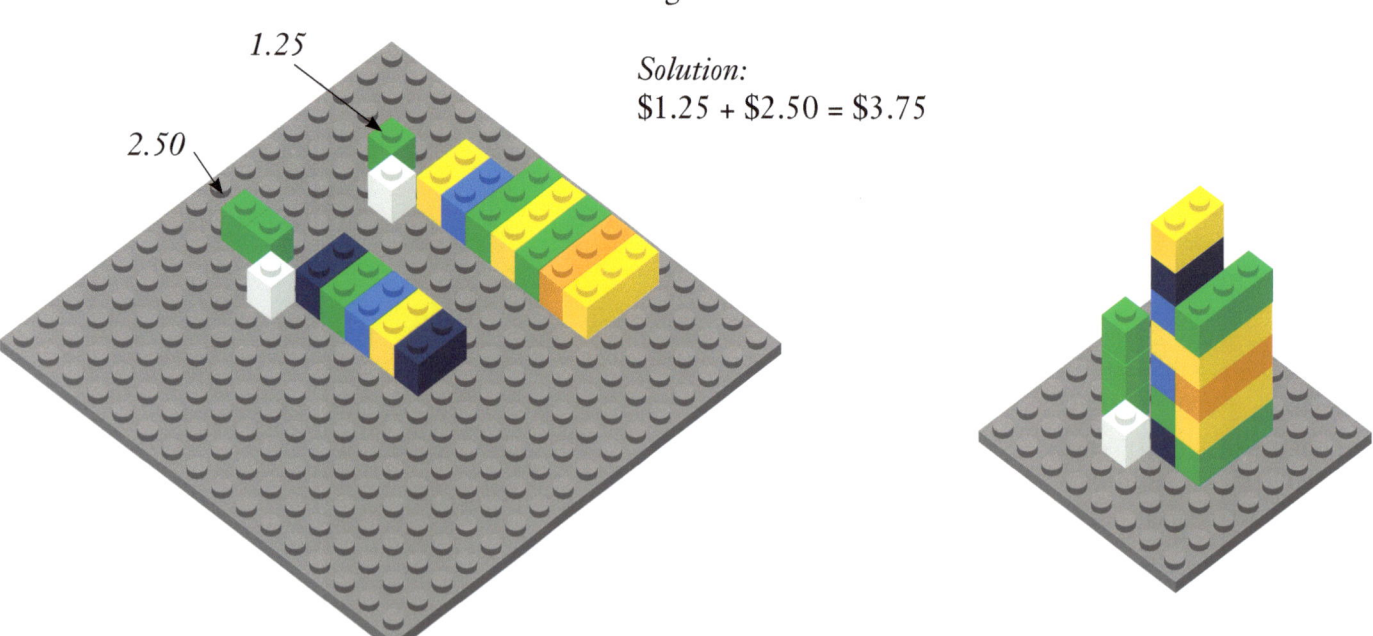

ADDING AND SUBTRACTING DECIMALS

SUGGESTED BRICKS

Size	Number
1x1	24
1x2	25
1x3	20
1x4	10
1x6	4
1x8	4
1x10	2
1x12	2
2x2	6
2x3	6
2x4	6

Note: Using a baseplate helps keep the bricks in place. One baseplate is suggested for these activities.

Students will learn/discover:
- How to model adding and subtracting decimals using the decimal grid system and the place value system
- How to decompose decimals

Why is this important?
Adding and subtracting decimals is relevant to real-life skills and activities, including the use of money when shopping. In learning to add and subtract decimal amounts, students build on their previously learned skills of addition and subtraction of whole numbers. Seeing decimals as part of a whole and in a place value format enables students to make connections between decimals, fractions, and whole numbers.

Vocabulary:
- **Decimal number:** A number with a fractional part represented by figures to the right of a decimal point; these figures are the numerator of the equivalent fraction, whose denominator is a power of ten (e.g., the decimal .2 is equivalent to $^2/_{10}$ or $^{20}/_{100}$)
- **Decimal notation:** A representation of a fraction or other real number using the base ten system, with any of the digits 0, 1, 2, 3, 4, 5, 6, 7, 8, 9, and a decimal point
- **Tenth:** One of 10 equal parts of a whole (10^{-1} or $^1/_{10}$ or .10); in decimal notation, the tenths place is the first place value position to the right of the decimal point

- **Hundredth:** One of 100 equal parts of a whole (10^{-2} or $1/100$ or .01); in decimal notation, the hundredths place is the second place value position to the right of the decimal point
- **Thousandth:** One of 1000 equal parts of a whole (10^{-3} or $1/1000$ or .001); in decimal notation, the thousandths place is the third place value position to the right of the decimal point
- **Expanded form:** A math sentence for a decimal number that shows all place value positions within the number (e.g., 1.25 = 1 + .20 + .05)
- **Addition:** The joining of two or more numerical values into a sum
- **Subtraction:** The calculation of the difference between two numerical values

How to use the companion student book, *Decimals Using LEGO® Bricks–Student Edition*:
- After students build their models, have them draw the models and explain their thinking in the Student Edition. Recording the models on paper after building them with bricks helps reinforce the concepts being taught.
- Discuss the vocabulary for each lesson with students as they work through the Student Edition.
- Use the chapter assessments in the Student Edition to gauge student understanding of the content.

Part 1: Show Them How

Review the definition of a decimal and what it represents (*answer:* like a fraction, a decimal is a form of notation used to represent a part of a whole). *Note:* It is important that students make the connection between decimal and fractional representations of parts of a whole.

Review how to model decimal amounts using the place value model and the decimal grid model (see Chapter 1).

Place value model:
1x2 brick = tenths place = $^1/_{10}$ = 0.1
1x3 brick = hundredths place = $^1/_{100}$ = 0.01
1x4 brick = thousandths place = $^1/_{1000}$ = 0.001
Note: Use a 1x1 brick to represent the decimal point. It is helpful to use the same brick color to represent the decimal point every time, especially when building mixed decimals (which also use 1x1 bricks to represent the place value for ones).

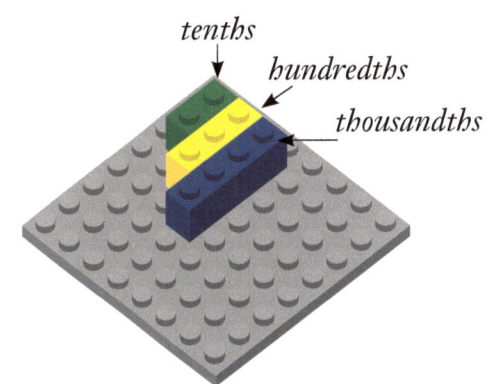

Decimal grid model:

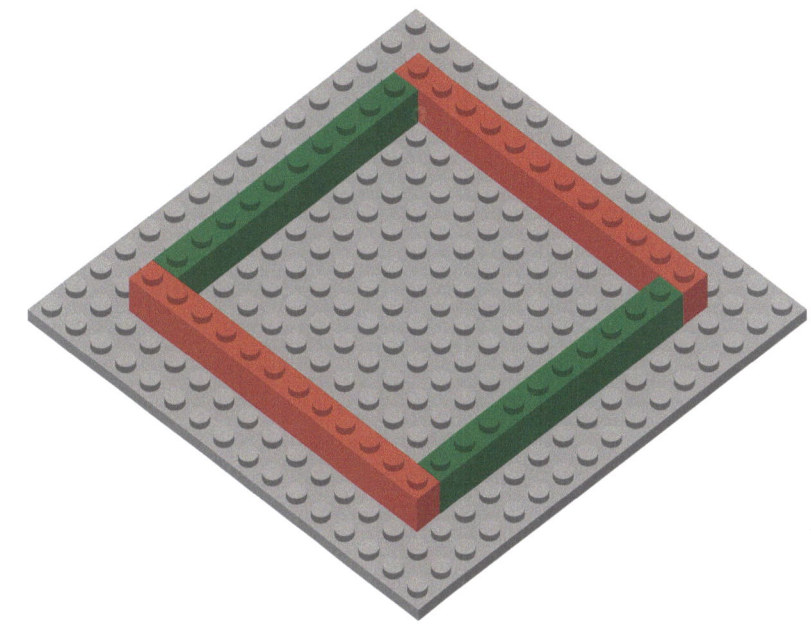

100 studs inside decimal grid

Problem #1: Build a decimal grid model to show the sum of 0.32 and 0.22.

1. Build a decimal grid.

2. Cover 32 studs in the grid with bricks of one color. Cover 22 more studs with bricks of another color. Have students build the same model. *Note:* Students may use a variety of brick sizes to model the total number of studs in each color.

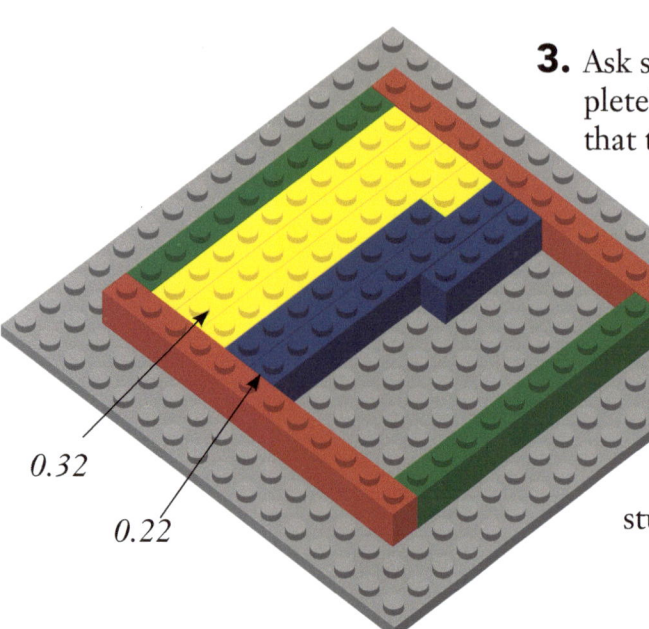

3. Ask students to count the number of 1x10 columns completely covered by bricks (*answer:* 5 columns). Explain that this is equivalent to the number of tenths.

4. Ask students to count the number of studs covered in the partially filled column (*answer:* 4 studs). Explain that this is equivalent to the number of hundredths.

5. Have students write an addition sentence for this problem (*answer:* 32 studs + 22 studs = 54 studs; or, 0.32 + 0.22 = 0.54).

Problem #2: Use a place value model to show two mixed decimals: 3.32 and 4.21. Show the sum of the two mixed decimals by stacking the bricks. Draw your model of the two mixed decimals and write a math sentence for the sum.

1. Build place value models for the two mixed decimals. Have students build the models along with you.

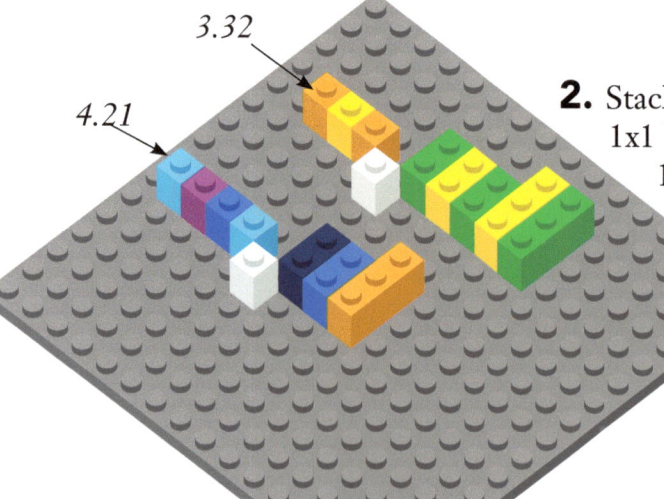

2. Stack the same-size bricks in the model of 3.32 (three 1x1 bricks stacked, three 1x2 bricks stacked, and two 1x3 bricks stacked).

3. Stack the bricks from the 4.21 model on top of the matching-sized bricks of the 3.32 model (four 1x1 bricks, two 1x2 bricks, and one 1x3 brick).

4. Count the number of bricks of each type in the combined model (*answer:* seven 1x1 bricks, five 1x2 bricks, and three 1x3 bricks). Have students identify the total amount represented by the model (*answer:* 7 wholes + 5 tenths + 3 hundredths = 7.53) and write the math sentence (*answer:* 3.32 + 4.21 = 7.53).

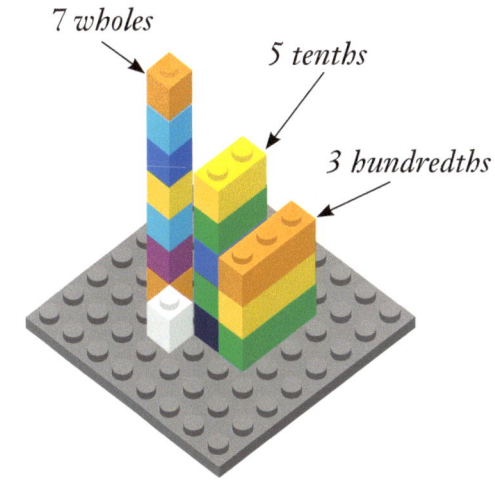

Problem #3: Build a model to show the difference between the decimals 0.54 and 0.32 (or 0.54 - 0.32)
Note: Explain to students that both the decimal grid model and the place value model work to model subtraction of decimals.

Decimal grid model:

1. Build a decimal grid.

2. Cover 54 studs in the grid with bricks of one color.

DR. SHIRLEY DISSELER | DECIMALS USING LEGO® BRICKS—TEACHER EDITION

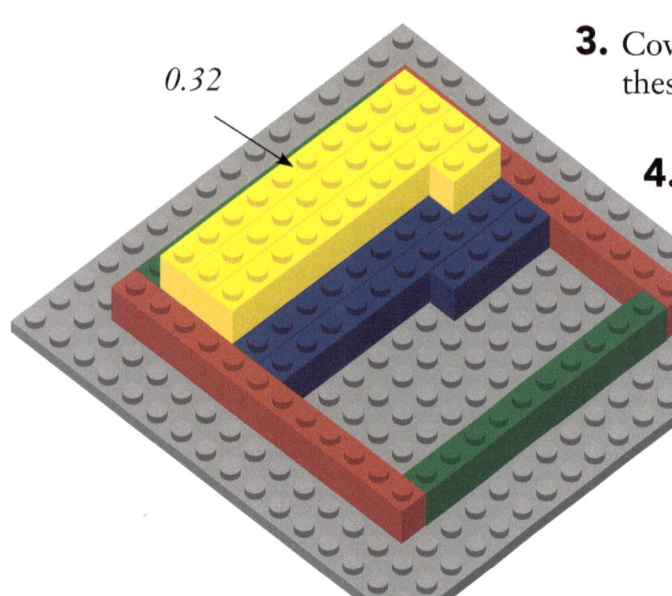

0.32

3. Cover 32 studs with bricks of another color, stacking these bricks **on top** of the first brick layer.

4. Ask students to count the number of studs in the bottom layer that are not covered by the top layer of bricks (*answer:* 22 studs). These bricks show the difference.

5. Have students write a math sentence for the problem (*answer:* 0.54 − 0.32 = 0.22).

Place value model:

1. Model each decimal number using the place value model.

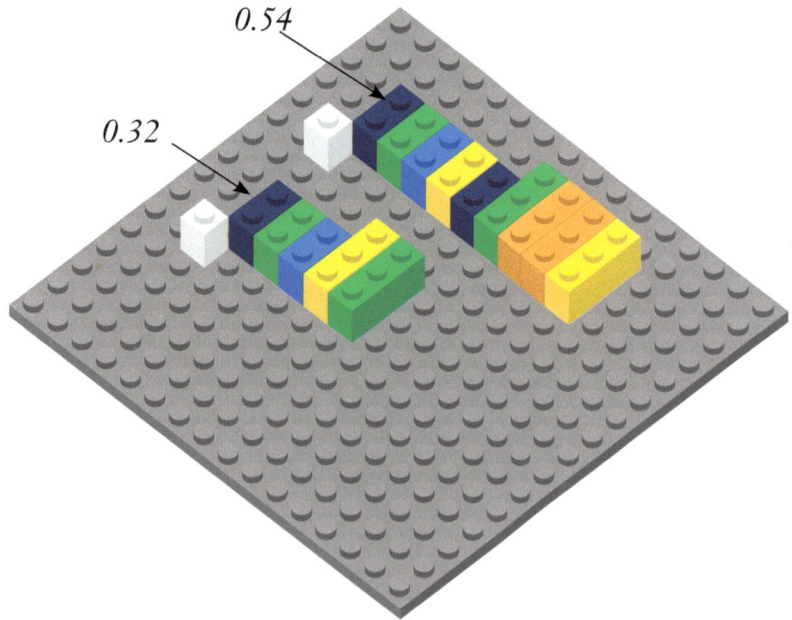

2. Ask students to identify the larger and the smaller decimal number (*answer:* 0.54 is the larger decimal number, and 0.32 is the smaller decimal number). Have students stack the three 1x2 bricks and two 1x3 bricks from the 0.32 model on top of the matching bricks in the 0.54 model.

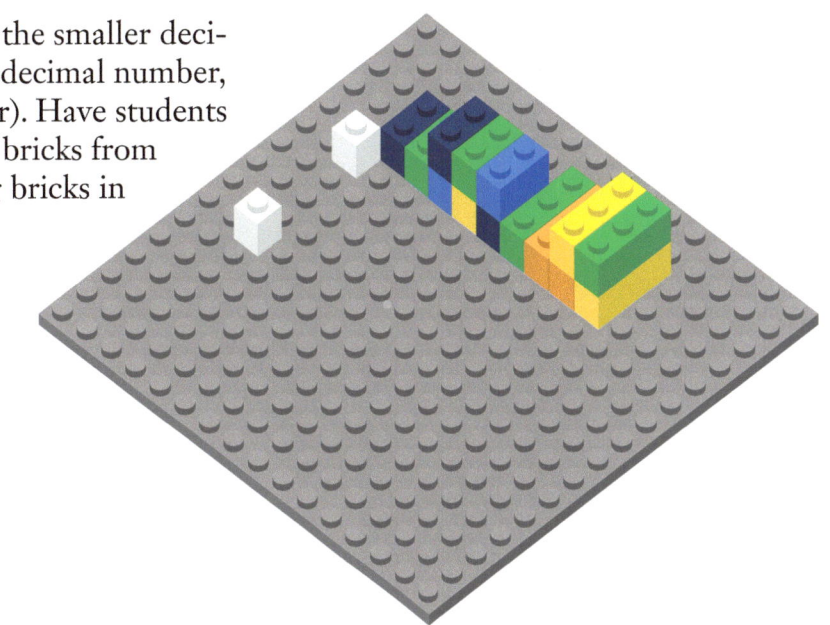

3. Remove all the bricks that are now in stacks (i.e., the three stacks of 1x2 bricks and two stacks of 1x3 bricks).

4. Explain to students that the remaining bricks in the model are equivalent to the difference between the two decimals. Have students identify the value of the remaining bricks and write a math sentence (*answer:* 0.54 - 0.32 = 0.22).

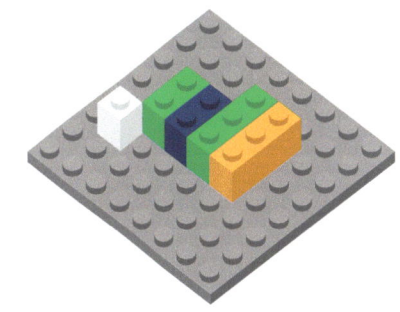

Problem #4: Build a place value model to show the difference between 0.53 and 0.14 (or 0.53 - 0.14).
Note: In this problem, students will explore decomposing decimals in order to subtract.

1. Have students build place value models for 0.53 and 0.14.

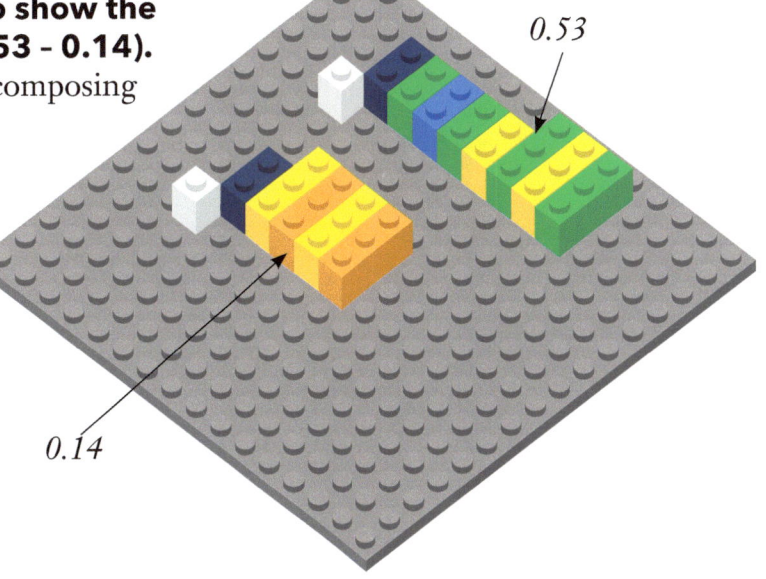

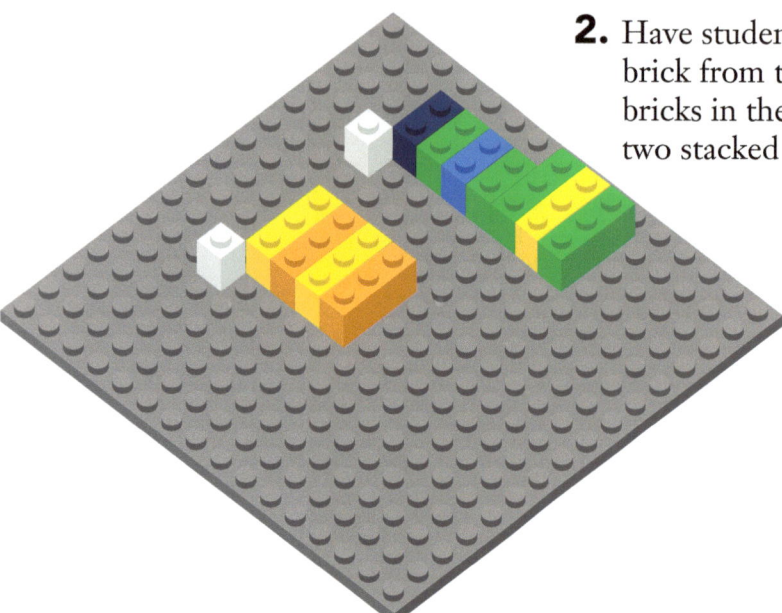

2. Have students stack the tenths, by placing the one 1x2 brick from the 0.14 model on top of one of the 1x2 bricks in the 0.53 model. Have students remove those two stacked 1x2 bricks from the model.

3. Explain to students that because there are only 3 hundredths in the larger number and 4 hundredths in the smaller number, it will require decomposing to subtract the two decimals. In the 0.53 decimal model, have students decompose 1 tenth into 10 hundredths by removing a 1x2 brick and replacing it with a stack of ten 1x3 bricks. The model now shows 13 hundredths (thirteen 1x3 bricks) and 3 tenths (three 1x2 bricks). *Note:* If there are not enough 1x3 bricks, use a combination of 1x2 and 1x1 bricks.

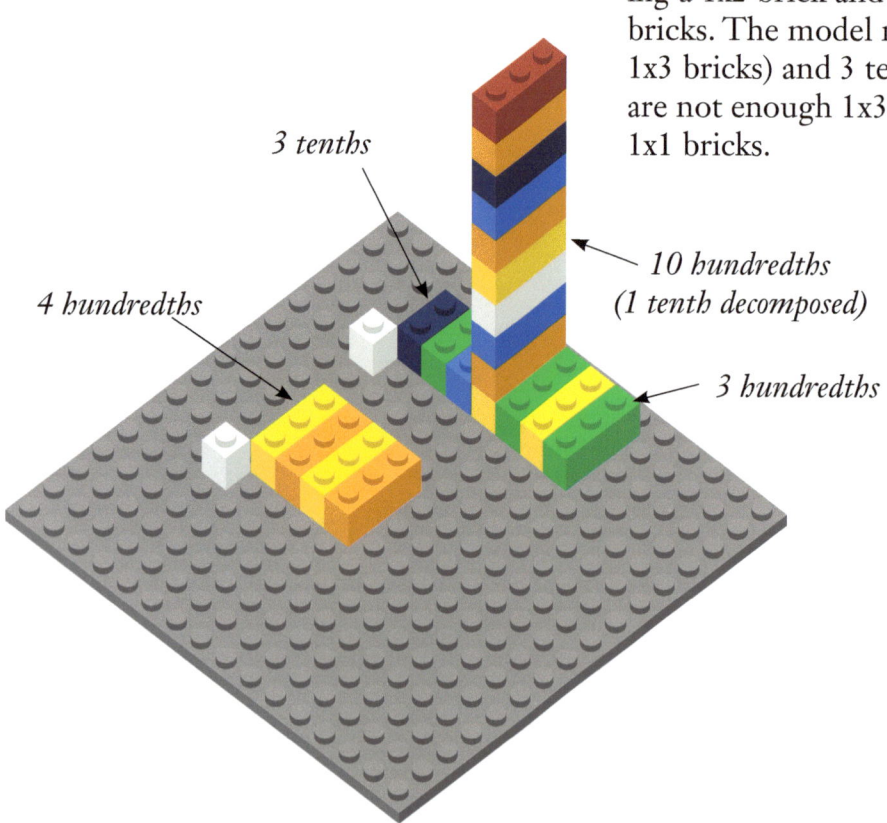

4. Ask students to identify the number of hundredths (1x3 bricks) left from the 0.14 decimal model (*answer:* 4 hundredths).

5. Have students stack the four remaining hundredths (1x3 bricks) from the 0.14 decimal model on top of the four columns of hundredths in the 0.53 model.

6. Have students remove pairs of stacked 1x3 bricks from the 0.53 model. *Note:* students should remove both 1x3 bricks in each of the small stacks, but only take two 1x3 bricks from the large stack.

7. Have students count the remaining bricks and identify the difference (*answer:* three 1x2 bricks and nine 1x3 bricks remain; the final difference is 3 tenths and 9 hundredths, or 0.39).

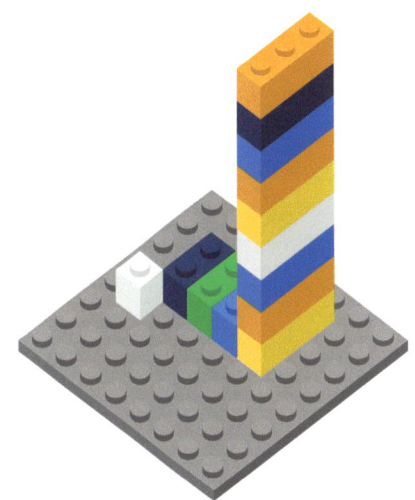

Part 2: Show What You Know

1. Can you build either a grid model or a place value model to show the difference between 0.41 and 0.27? Draw the solution and explain your thinking. Write a math sentence for your solution.

Grid model possible solution:

0.41 - 0.27 = 0.14

41 studs covered shows 41 out of 100. Subtract 27 by covering 27 studs with a new layer of bricks in a different color. 14 of the first 41 studs are uncovered, which shows 0.14 of 1.00.

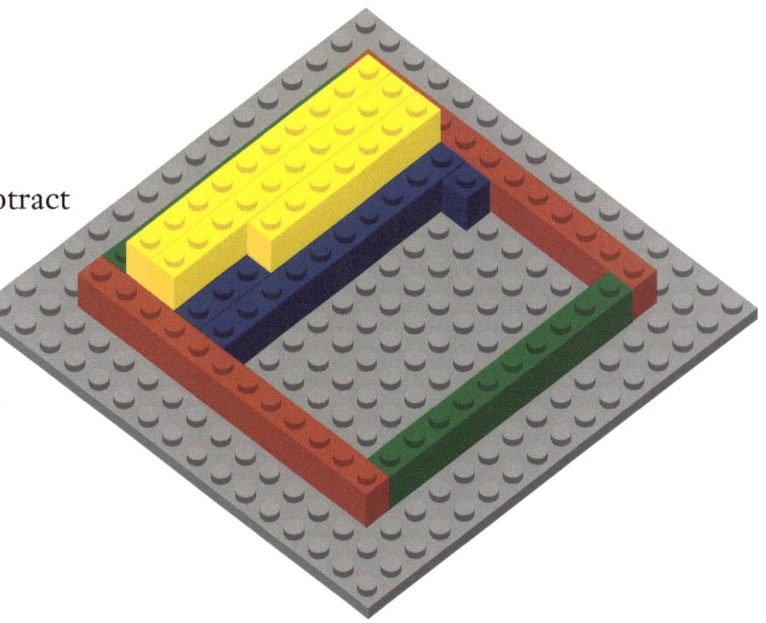

Place value model possible solution:

Note: Using the place value system, students will need to decompose and regroup the decimals.

Build place value models for the two decimal numbers.

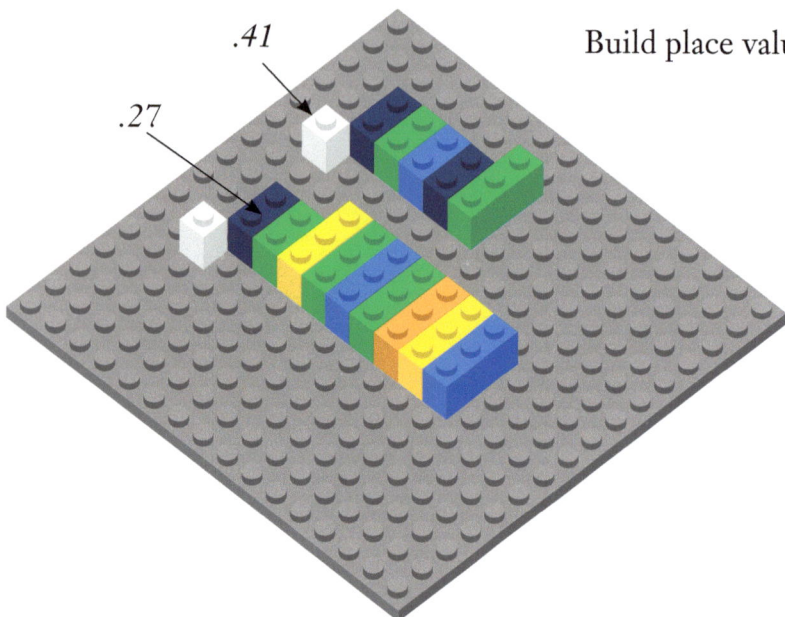

Stack two 1x2 bricks (tenths) from the model of 0.27 on two 1x2 bricks from the model of 0.41, then remove both sets of 1x2 bricks.

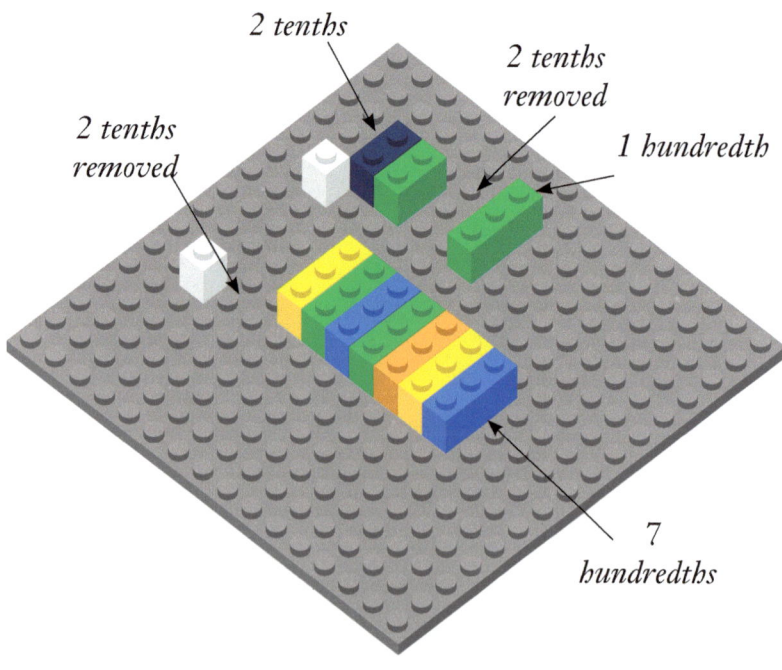

50 DECIMALS USING LEGO® BRICKS—TEACHER EDITION | DR. SHIRLEY DISSELER

Decompose one tenth from the top model into ten hundredths by removing one 1x2 brick and adding a stack of ten 1x3 bricks to the existing 1x3 brick to show 11 hundredths.

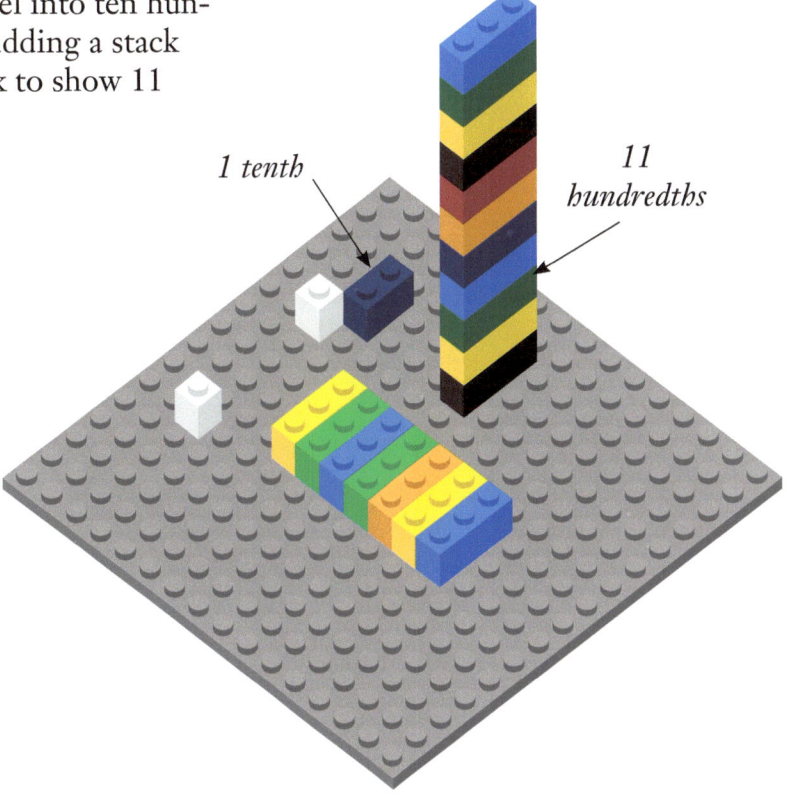

Match each 1x3 brick (hundredth) from the bottom model with a 1x3 brick from the top model, and remove the matching pairs. One 1x2 (one tenth) and four 1x3 bricks (four hundredths) remain, or 0.14.

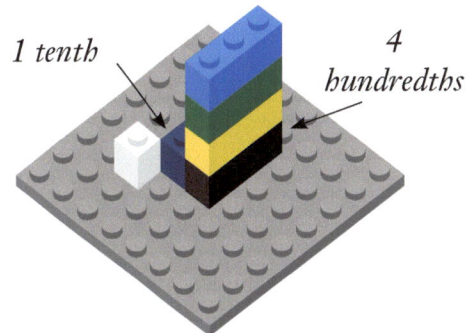

2. Can you build a grid model that shows the sum of 0.15 and 0.23? Draw your solution and write a math sentence. Label each decimal.

Possible solution:

0.15 + 0.23 = 0.38

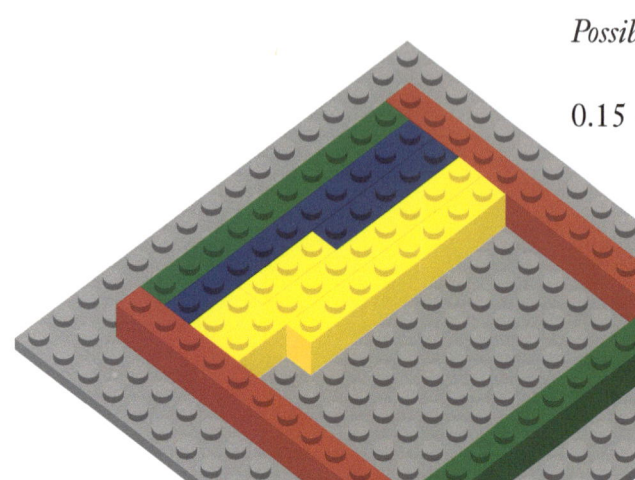

The model shows that 0.15 + 0.23 is equivalent to 0.38 because 38 out of 100 studs in the grid are covered.

3. Can you build a grid model or a place value model that shows the sum of 0.12, 0.23, and 0.4? Draw and label the decimals in your model. Write a math sentence for your solution.

Grid model possible solution:

0.12 + 0.23 + 0.4 = 0.75

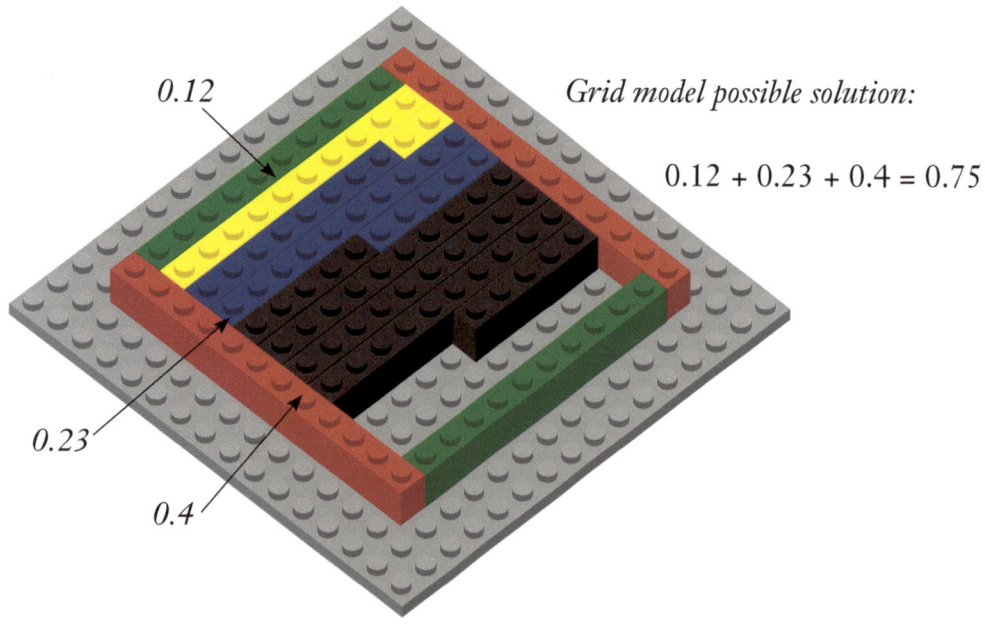

Place value model possible solution:

0.12 + 0.23 + 0.4 = 0.75

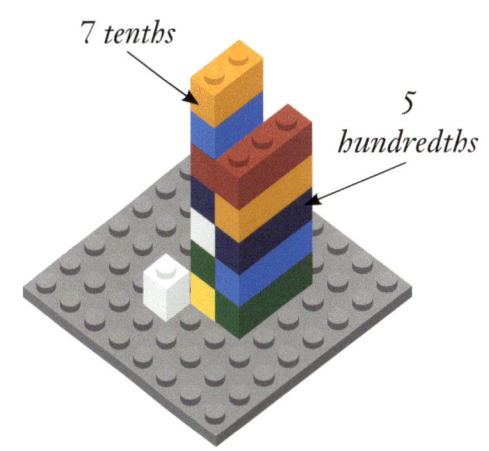

7 tenths

5 hundredths

4. Can you build a grid model to show the difference between 0.4 and 0.32? Draw and explain your model, and write a math sentence for your solution.

Possible solution:

0.4 - 0.32 = 0.08

40 out of 100 studs are covered to represent 0.40. Thirty-two studs in another color cover the 40 studs, leaving 8 studs uncovered. This represents the difference between the two decimal numbers. These are 8 studs out of 100, or 0.08 out of 1.00, since each stud on the baseplate represents one hundredth.

6

SUGGESTED BRICKS

Size	Number
1x1	24
1x2	25
1x3	12
1x4	10
1x6	4
1x8	4
1x10	2
1x12	2
2x2	8
2x3	6
2x4	6

Note: Using a baseplate helps keep the bricks in place. Two baseplates are suggested for these activities.

MULTIPLYING DECIMALS

Students will learn/discover:
- How to multiply whole numbers by decimals
- How to multiply decimals by decimals to the tenths place
- How to multiply mixed decimals by decimals to the tenths place
- How to use a place value model for decimal multiplication
- How to use a grid model for decimal multiplication
- How to use a discovering wholes model for decimal multiplication
- How to use an array model for decimal multiplication

Why is this important?
Multiplying decimals is an extension of whole number multiplication and addition, and relevant to real-world situations involving such topics as money, medicine, and distance. Multiplying decimals is similar to multiplying whole numbers, although students often struggle with this concept. Students tend to think that decimal syntax changes the nature of a multiplication problem, when in fact it only changes the answer to the problem.

Vocabulary:
- **Decimal number:** A number with a fractional part represented by figures to the right of a decimal point; these figures are the numerator of the equivalent fraction, whose denominator is a power of ten (e.g., the decimal .2 is equivalent to $^2/_{10}$ or $^{20}/_{100}$)
- **Decimal notation:** A representation of a fraction or other real number using the base ten system, with any of the digits 0, 1, 2, 3, 4, 5, 6, 7, 8, 9, and a decimal point

- **Tenth:** One of 10 equal parts of a whole (10^{-1} or $1/10$ or .10); in decimal notation, the tenths place is the first place value position to the right of the decimal point
- **Hundredth:** One of 100 equal parts of a whole (10^{-2} or $1/100$ or .01); in decimal notation, the hundredths place is the second place value position to the right of the decimal point
- **Thousandth:** One of 1000 equal parts of a whole (10^{-3} or $1/1000$ or .001); in decimal notation, the thousandths place is the third place value position to the right of the decimal point
- **Multiplying:** Repeated addition of the same number for a defined number of sets (e.g., 3 x 4 = 4 repeated 3 times, or 3 sets of 4)
- **Multiplicand:** The number in a set, to be multiplied by the multiplier (e.g., in 3 x 4, the number 4 is the multiplicand; 3 x 4 = 3 sets of 4)
- **Multiplier:** The number of times a set is repeated (e.g., in 3 x 4, the number 3 is the multiplier; 3 x 4 = 3 sets of 4)

How to use the companion student book, *Decimals Using LEGO® Bricks—Student Edition*:
- After students build their models, have them draw the models and explain their thinking in the Student Edition. Recording the models on paper after building them with bricks helps reinforce the concepts being taught.
- Discuss the vocabulary for each lesson with students as they work through the Student Edition.
- Use the chapter assessments in the Student Edition to gauge student understanding of the content.

Part 1: Show Them How

In this chapter, students will learn how to multiply decimal parts of a whole.

Review the definition of a decimal and what it represents (*answer:* like a fraction, a decimal is a form of notation used to represent a part of a whole). *Note:* It is important that students make the connection between the decimal and the fractional representations of parts of a whole.

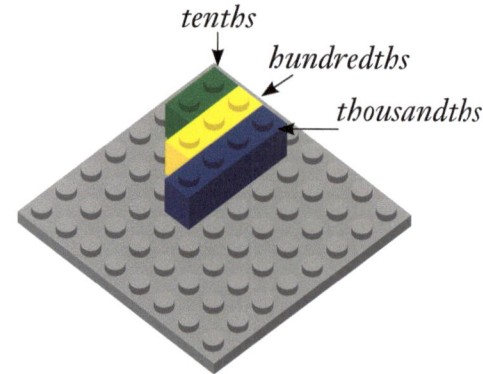

Multiplying a Decimal by a Whole Number Using a Place Value Model

Note: If necessary, review with students how to model decimal amounts using the place value modeling process (Chapter 1).

1x2 brick = tenths place = $1/10$ = 0.1
1x3 brick = hundredths place = $1/100$ = 0.01
1x4 brick = thousandths place = $1/1000$ = 0.001

Note: Use a 1x1 brick to represent the decimal point. It is helpful to use the same brick color to represent the decimal point every time, especially when building mixed decimals (which also use 1x1 bricks to represent the place value for ones).

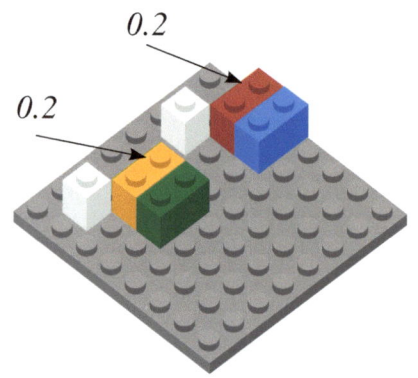

Problem #1: Model the multiplication of 0.2 by 2 using bricks to model place values.

Note: Use a place value model to show multiplication of a decimal by a whole number.

1. Have students build two decimal place value models of 0.2.

2. Ask students how to write a math sentence for this multiplication problem (*answer:* 2 x 0.2). Remind students that multiplication involves repeated addition of the same number for a defined number of sets. Ask students how many sets of 0.2 are modeled (*answer:* two sets).

3. Show students how to model repeated addition with bricks, by making a single stack of all the 1x2 bricks.

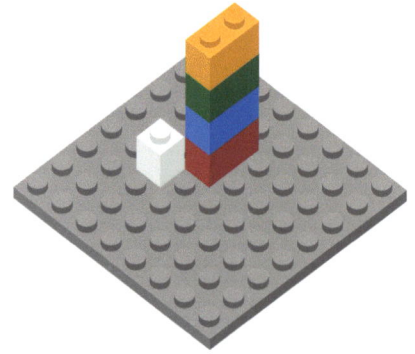

4. Have students unstack the model and arrange the 1x2 bricks into a single place value model. Ask students to identify the number of 1x2 bricks in the model, and the decimal amount (*answer:* four 1x2 bricks, or 0.4).

Problem #2: Using a place value model, find the product for: 3 x 0.4

1. Have students identify the multiplier and the multiplicand (*answer:* multiplier is 3 and multiplicand is 0.4, which means that 3 x 0.4 is three sets of 0.4). Have students build three models of 0.4.

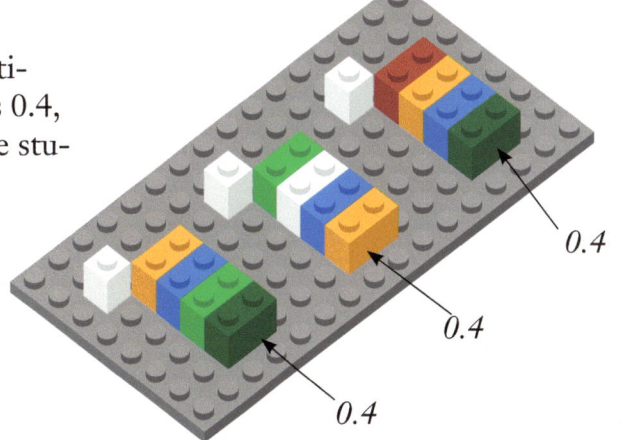

2. Have students place all the 1x2 bricks into a single stack. Ask students how many 1x2 bricks are in the stack (*answer:* 12 bricks).

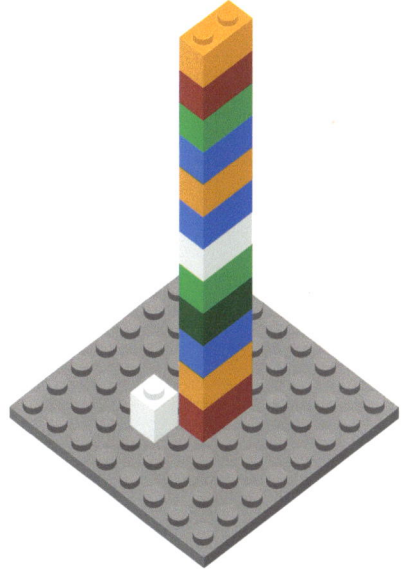

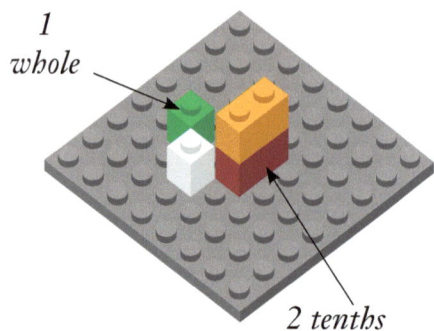

1 whole

2 tenths

3. Ask students to identify the number of tenths in one whole (*answer:* 10 tenths). Explain that since there are twelve 1x2 bricks in the model (each representing one tenth), students can decompose 10 of the 1x2 bricks into a 1x1 brick to show one whole. Have students remove 10 of the 1x2 bricks from the tenths place, and add a 1x1 brick to the ones place (to the left of the decimal point).

4. Have students identify the bricks now in the model, and the mixed decimal represented (*answer:* one 1x1 brick and two 1x2 bricks are in the model, representing 1.2).

Multiplying a Decimal by a Decimal Using a Decimal Grid Model

Note: If necessary, review how to model decimal amounts using the decimal grid modeling process (Chapter 1).

Note: A decimal grid model is used to model multiplication of a decimal by another decimal.

Problem #3: Using a decimal grid model, find the product for: 0.3 x 0.4

1. Ask students to describe the difference between 3 x 0.4 (Problem #2) and 0.3 x 0.4 (*answer:* in 3 x 0.4, the multiplier 3 is a whole number, while in 0.3 x 0.4, the multiplier 0.3 is a decimal).

2. Have students build a decimal grid (see Chapter 1).

3. Have students cover 30 studs vertically inside the grid with the same color brick. Use three 1x10 bricks if available, or any combination of bricks to create this 3 x 10-stud configuration. Explain that these bricks represent the decimal 0.3, which is the multiplier.

30 studs = 0.3 or 3 tenths

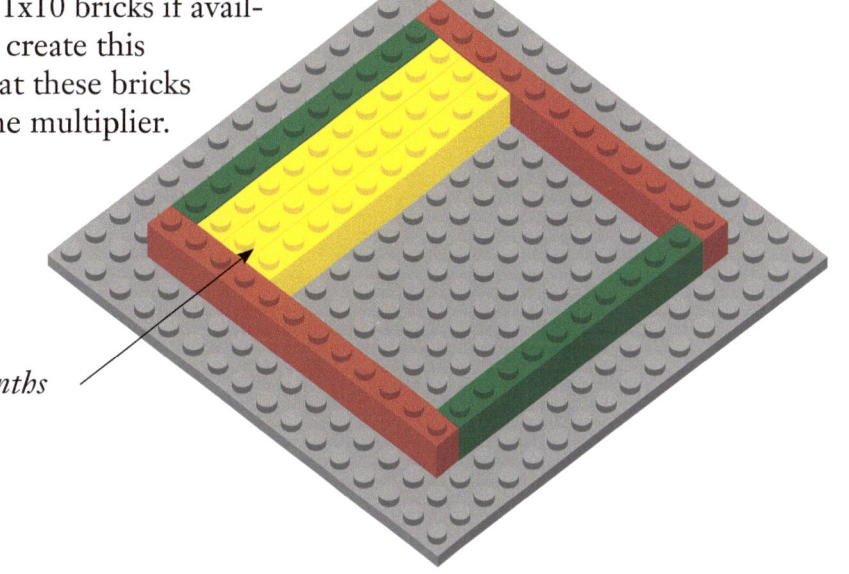

4. Have students model 0.4 (the multiplicand) by placing 40 studs of a different color horizontally on the same grid. *Note:* Bricks that overlap with the original 30 should be placed on top of the vertical layer.

5. Have students identify the number of new studs that overlap with the original 30 studs (*answer:* 12 studs). Ask students what decimal is represented by the overlapping studs (12 hundredths, or 0.12).

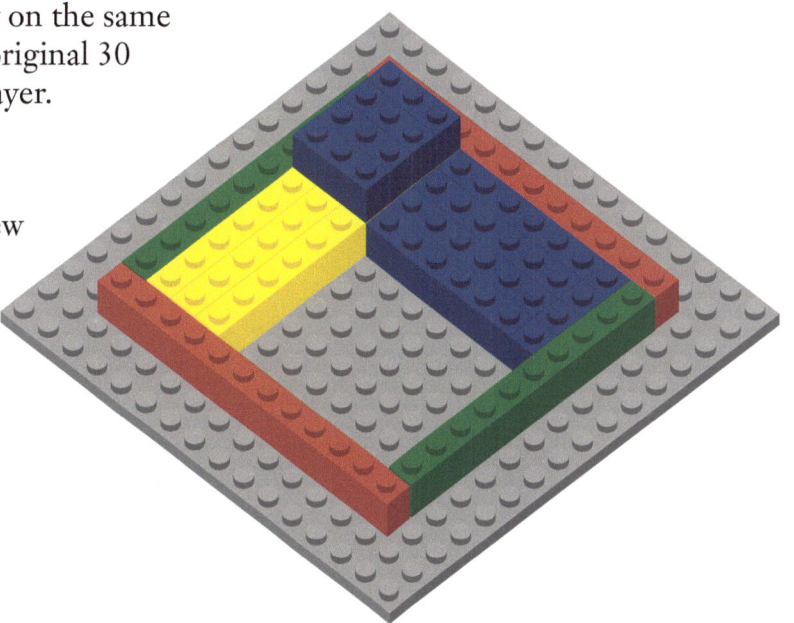

Problem #4: Multiply 0.3 x 0.2 using a decimal grid model.

1. Build a decimal grid on a baseplate (see Chapter 1). Have students build the same decimal grid.

2. Model 0.3 (the multiplier) with three 1x10 bricks placed vertically in the grid. These bricks represent 3 sets of tenths. Use three 1x10 bricks if available, or a combination of smaller bricks.

3. Model multiplication by 0.2 (the multiplicand) by placing 20 studs horizontally across the 30 bricks representing 0.3. Show the overlapping bricks on the top layer.

4. Ask students how many studs are used in both decimals (*answer:* 6). Since each stud is .01 of the whole, the model shows that the answer is 0.06.

60   DECIMALS USING LEGO® BRICKS—TEACHER EDITION | DR. SHIRLEY DISSELER

Multiplying a Whole Number or Mixed Decimal by a Decimal Using a Discovering Wholes Model

Explain to students that they will learn a third type of model to show the multiplication of a whole number or mixed decimal by a decimal. This discovering wholes model uses the format of an array (see *Multiplication Using LEGO® Bricks*).

Problem #5: Find the product of 3.0 x 0.4 using the discovering wholes model.

1. Use 1x2 bricks (representing tenths) to build an array of three sets of 0.4. Have students build the same model. *Note:* Be sure students understand that each 1x2 brick represents one tenth, or 0.1.

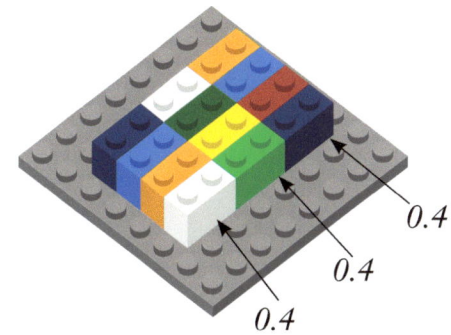

2. Have students choose a brick color to represent the whole (in this example, the whole is represented with yellow bricks). Ask students how many 1x2 bricks, or sets of two studs that represent tenths, are equal to one whole (*answer:* ten 1x2 bricks or 10 sets of two studs). Add ten 1x2 bricks of that color to the model, stacking them on top of the first layer to model one whole (10 tenths).

3. Have students count the number of 1x2 bricks in the original layer that remain uncovered, and identify the number of tenths represented (*answer:* two 1x2 bricks, or 2 tenths).

   Have students identify the solution to 3.0 x 0.4 represented by the model (*answer:* 1 whole and 2 tenths, or 1.2).

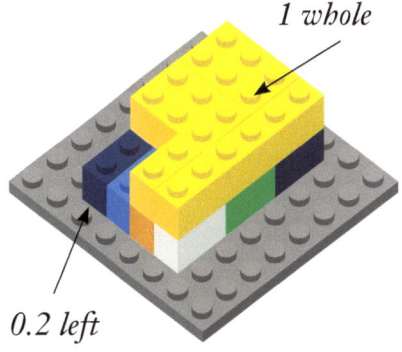

Problem #6: Find the product of 1.2 x 0.4.
Note: This problem is a mixed decimal multiplied by a decimal.

1. Explain to students that the first number (1.2) is the multiplier, and indicates how many sets of the second number will be created (1.2 sets). The second number (0.4) is the multiplicand, and indicates the size of each set (a set of 0.4).

2. Have students break the multiplier of 1.2 into its component parts (*answer:* 1.0 + 0.2). Show students how to break down the multiplication problem of 1.2 x 0.4 into two problems, one for each of the component parts (*answer:* 1.0 x 0.4 and 0.2 x 0.4). *Note:* This is an example of the distributive property.

10 x 4 array models 0.4

3. Model the solution to 1.0 x 0.4 as if the bricks are in the decimal grid.

Have students build a 10 x 4 array to represent the solution (*answer:* 40 studs, or 0.4).

4. Using another baseplate, have students model the solution to 0.2 x 0.4 on a decimal grid (*answer:* 8 studs, or 0.08).

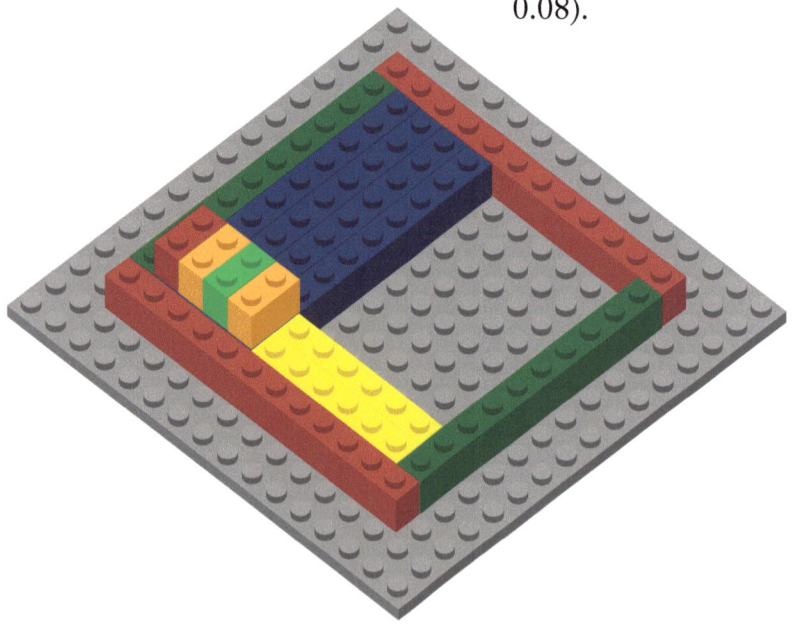

Decimal grid model of 0.2 x 0.4 = .08

5. Transfer the resulting 2 x 4 array, which represents the number of studs in 0.2 x 0.4 (0.08), to the baseplate with the 40 studs that model 1 x 0.4 = 0.4. Have students add the number of studs in each model to find the total number of studs (*answer:* 40 + 8 = 48).

Ask students to identify the decimal represented by 48 studs (*answer:* 48 studs = 48 out of 100 studs = 4 tenths and 8 hundredths = 0.48).

0.2 x 0.4 = 2 studs x 4 studs, or 2 sets of 4 studs = 8 studs
8 studs = 0.08

1.0 x 0.4 = 10 studs x 4 studs, or 10 sets of 4 studs = 40 studs
40 studs = 0.4

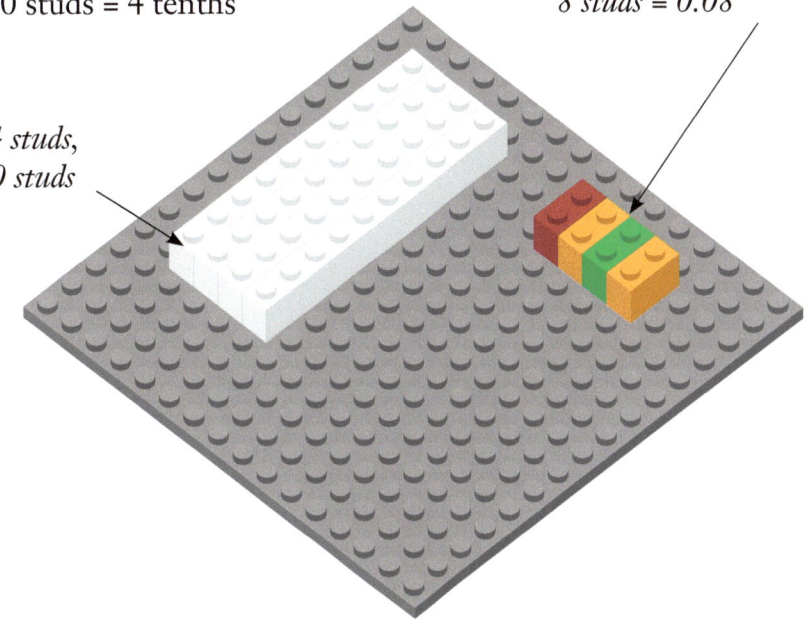

40 studs + 8 studs = 48 studs

Part 2: Show What You Know

1. Can you build a place value model to show the solution to the multiplication problem 2 x 0.6? Draw your model and label the parts of the decimal. Explain your thinking, and write a math sentence for the solution.

Possible solution:

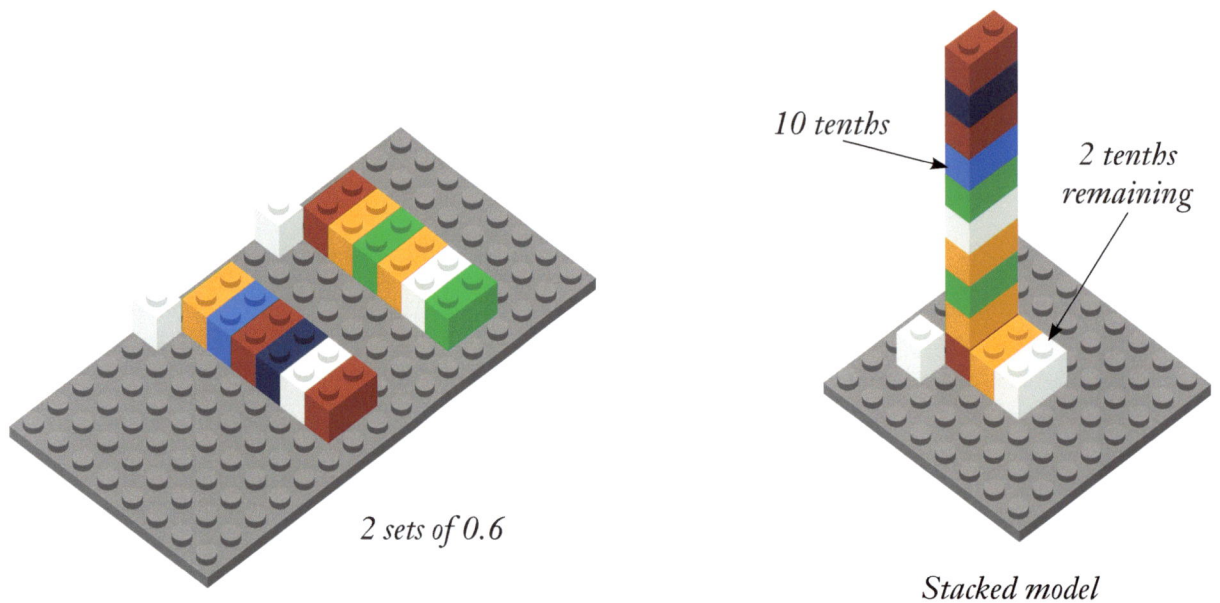

2 sets of 0.6

Stacked model

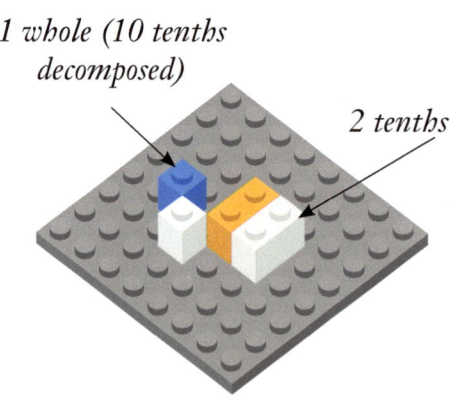

1 whole + 2 tenths = 1.2
Math sentence: 2 x 0.6 = 1.2

64 DECIMALS USING LEGO® BRICKS—TEACHER EDITION | DR. SHIRLEY DISSELER

2. Can you build a decimal grid model to show the solution to the multiplication problem 0.2 x 0.5? Draw your model and label the parts of the decimal. Explain your thinking, and write a math sentence for the solution.

Possible solution:

0.5 = 50 studs

Overlap = 10 studs = 0.1

0.2 = 20 studs

$$0.2 \times 0.5 = 0.10$$

3. Can you build a model to show the solution to the multiplication problem 1.3 x 0.3? *Hint:* Remember to break the problem apart into two component parts using the distributive property. Draw your model and label the parts of the decimal. Explain your thinking, and write a math sentence for the solution.

Possible solution:

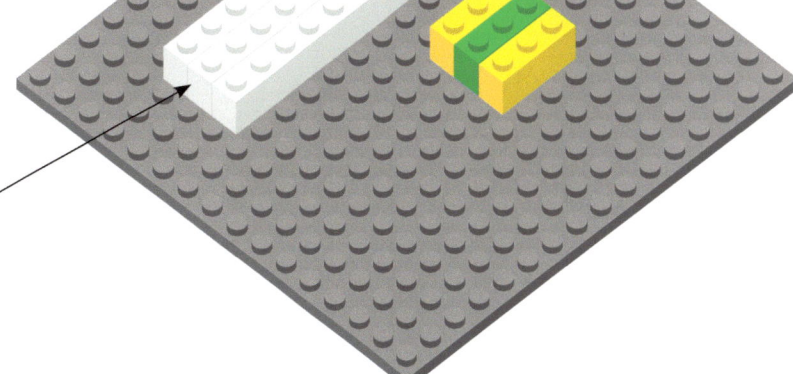

0.3 x 0.3 = 3 studs x 3 studs = 9 studs
9 studs = 0.09
0.3 x 0.3 = 0.09

1.0 x 0.3 = 10 studs x 3 studs = 30 studs
30 studs = 0.3
1.0 x 0.3 = 0.3

30 studs + 9 studs, or 0.3 + 0.09 = 39 studs out of 100, or 0.39
math sentence: 1.3 x 0.3 = 0.39

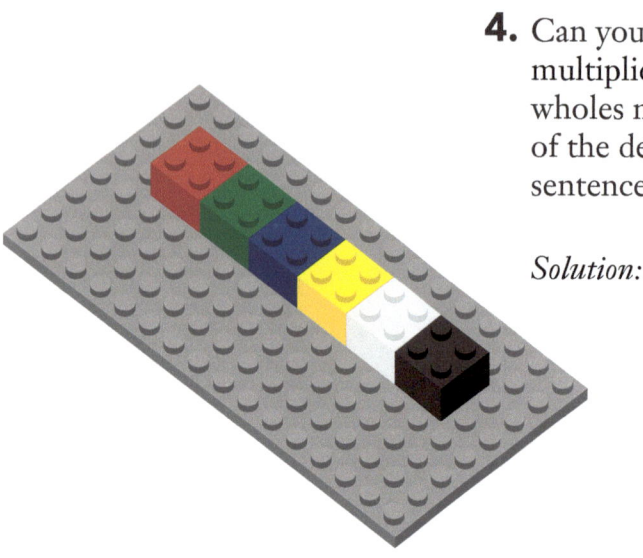

4. Can you build a model to show the solution to the multiplication problem 6.0 x 0.2, using the discovering wholes method? Draw your model and label the parts of the decimal. Explain your thinking, and write a math sentence for the solution.

Solution:

6 sets of 0.2 (2 studs represent 0.1, so 4 studs represent 0.2)

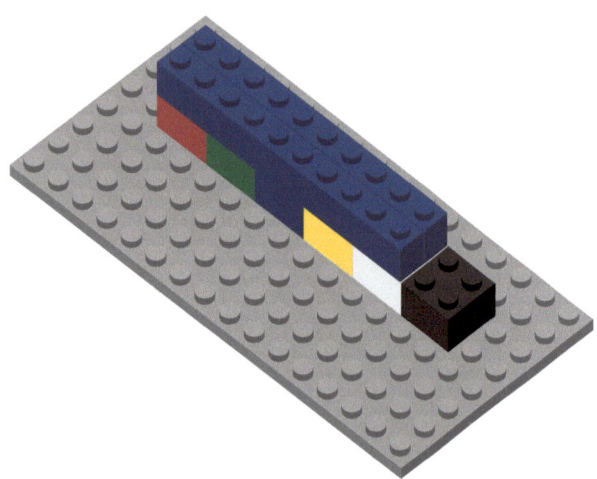

20 studs = 10 tenths or one whole (1.0)
4 studs remaining = two tenths (0.2)
1.0 + 0.2 = 1.2
math sentence: 6.0 x 0.2 = 1.2

DIVIDING WHOLE AND MIXED NUMBERS BY DECIMALS USING A GRID MODEL

SUGGESTED BRICKS

Size	Number
1x1	60
1x2	25
1x3	12
1x4	10
1x6	4
1x8	4
1x10	2
1x12	2
2x2	6
2x3	6
2x4	6

Note: Using a baseplate helps keep the bricks in place. One baseplate is suggested for these activities.

Students will learn/discover:
- How to divide a whole number by a decimal
- How to divide mixed decimals by a decimal
- How to model decimal division using a grid model

Why is this important?
Dividing decimals is an important skill that naturally progresses from division of whole numbers and should be approached in the same manner. In everyday life, students will need to divide decimals when handling money or calculating time. Students should also relate the division of decimals to fractions as they learn to use equal groups with fractional parts in a decimal format.

Vocabulary:
- **Decimal number:** A number with a fractional part represented by figures to the right of a decimal point; these figures are the numerator of the equivalent fraction, whose denominator is a power of ten (e.g., the decimal .2 is equivalent to $^2/_{10}$ or $^{20}/_{100}$)

- **Decimal notation:** A representation of a fraction or other real number using the base ten system, with any of the digits 0, 1, 2, 3, 4, 5, 6, 7, 8, 9, and a decimal point
- **Mixed decimal:** A decimal value that includes a whole number and a decimal portion of another whole (e.g., 3.2 means 3 wholes and 2 tenths of another whole)
- **Tenth:** One of ten equal parts of a whole (10^{-1} or $1/10$ or .10); in decimal notation, the tenths place is the first place value position to the right of the decimal point
- **Hundredth:** One of 100 equal parts of a whole (10^{-2} or $1/100$ or .01); in decimal notation, the hundredths place is the second place value position to the right of the decimal point
- **Thousandth:** One of 1000 equal parts of a whole (10^{-3} or $1/1000$ or .001); in decimal notation, the thousandths place is the third place value position to the right of the decimal point
- **Quotitive division:** The process of repeated subtraction of the same number at each iteration
- **Partitive (equal groups) division:** The process of partitioning a given amount into equal groups
- **Quotient:** The answer to a division problem
- **Dividend:** The number being divided
- **Divisor:** The number of sets into which the dividend is being divided

How to use the companion student book, *Decimals Using LEGO® Bricks–Student Edition*:
- After students build their models, have them draw the models and explain their thinking in the Student Edition. Recording the models on paper after building them with bricks helps reinforce the concepts being taught.
- Discuss the vocabulary for each lesson with students as they work through the Student Edition.
- Use the chapter assessments in the Student Edition to gauge student understanding of the content.

Part 1: Show Them How

Review the definition of a decimal and what it represents (*answer:* like a fraction, a decimal is a form of notation used to represent a part of a whole). *Note:* It is important that students make the connection between decimal and fractional representations of parts of a whole.

Review the definition of division (*answer:* division is the breaking apart of a number into equal groups). The process of division can be thought of in two ways: as *partitive*, where a given amount is partitioned into equal groups (also called *equal groups* division); and *quotitive*, where *repeated subtraction* is used to find the number of groups.

Explain to students that division of decimals follows the same general practice as division of fractions: the quotient is usually larger than the dividend or the divisor because the quotient refers to groups or sets.

Remind students that bricks can be used in many representational ways. In this lesson, the strategy utilized is the decimal grid model. This strategy uses a 10 x 10 rectangular grid with 100 studs inside. When used to model addition, subtraction, and multiplication of decimals, the grid represents 1 whole. But when dividing whole numbers by decimals, the studs within the grid represent different values during the process.

Guide students to build a 10 x 10 decimal grid using two 1x12 bricks and two 1x10 bricks. Be sure there are 100 studs showing on the baseplate inside the grid.

DR. SHIRLEY DISSELER | DECIMALS USING LEGO® BRICKS—TEACHER EDITION

Problem #1: Solve the division problem: 2.0 ÷ 0.2

Note: In this problem, the decimal grid is used a bit differently than in previous chapters. Here, each 1x10 strip of studs represents 1 whole. To model 2.0 (the dividend) in this problem, place two 1x10 bricks inside the decimal grid.

1. Explain that 2.0 is the dividend (the number being divided), and 0.2 is the divisor (the number of sets into which the dividend is being divided).

The dividend will show how many 1x10 bricks to use to model that number.

The divisor will show which brick to use to find the total number of wholes in the solution.

2. Explain that the place value of the divisor can be used to describe the dividend. Ask students to name the place value of the divisor 0.2 (*answer:* tenths). The number of tenths in the divisor (2 tenths) shows which brick to use to model the divisor (a 1x2 brick). *Note:* If the divisor were 0.3, a 1x3 brick would be used to model it.

3. In this decimal grid, one tenth is modeled by one stud. Therefore, one whole is modeled by 10 studs. Two wholes, or 2.0 (the dividend), is modeled by two sets of 10 studs.

Build a decimal grid, then model the dividend by placing two 1x10 bricks on the decimal grid. Explain that these bricks represent 2.0, or two sets of 10 tenths. Have students build the same model and draw it.

2 wholes

4. To model the division of 2 by 0.2, cover the two 1x10 bricks with 1x2 bricks. *Note:* Make sure that students understand that each stud represents one tenth, so each 1x2 brick represents two tenths, or 0.2, in this model. Have students build the same model.

5. Have students count the number of 1x2 bricks on the model (*answer:* ten 1x2 bricks). Explain that this shows 2.0 ÷ 0.2 is equal to 10 sets of 0.2.

6. Have students draw their models and write a math sentence for the solution (*answer:* 2 ÷ 0.2 = 10).

Note: Students might try to build two 100-stud decimal grids and divide by whole rows of 2 tenths. Discourage students from using this method, as it will take a lot of bricks and time.

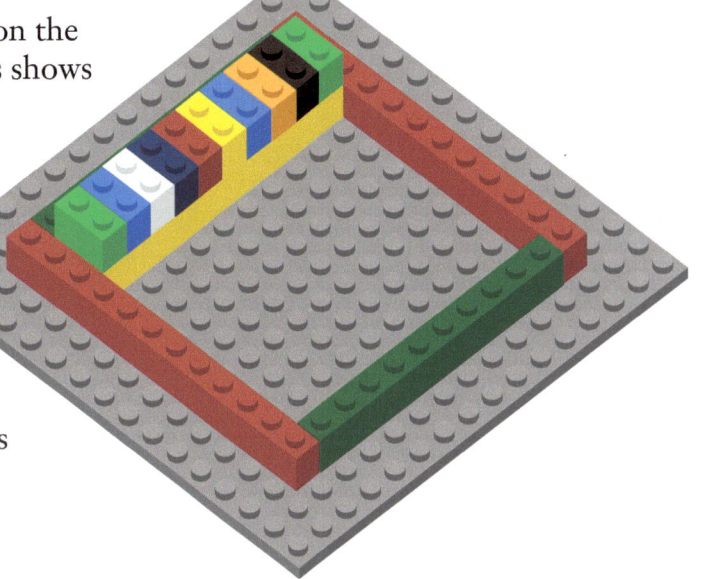

Problem #2: Solve the division problem: 6.0 ÷ 0.3

1. Explain that 6.0 is the dividend (the number being divided) and 0.3 is the divisor (the number in each set when the dividend is separated into equal groups).

The dividend will show how many 1x10 bricks to use to model that number.

The divisor will show which brick to use to find the total number of wholes in the solution.

2. Have students build a model of 6.0 with 6 sets of 10 studs, and then draw and label it.

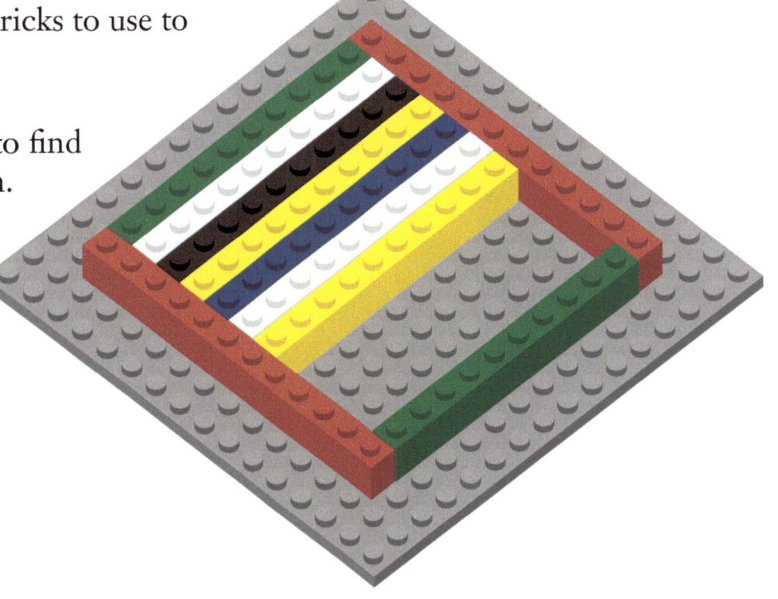

3. Ask students what brick to use to model the division based on the number of tenths in the divisor of 0.3 (*answer:* a 1x3 brick, since there are 3 tenths in 0.3). Ask students to model the sets of 3 tenths in 6.0 using 1x3 bricks. *Note:* Remind students that because each stud is 0.1, three studs represent 0.3.

4. Have students cover the 6 sets of 10 studs in the grid with 1x3 bricks and count the number of 1x3 bricks used (*answer:* 20). Have students draw the outline of each set of 3 studs on their drawing of the model and label the drawing.

5. Have students write a math sentence for the model (*answer:* 6.0 ÷ 0.3 = 20 sets of 0.3).

Problem #3: Solve the division problem: 7.0 ÷ 0.3

Note: In this problem, students will see how to use a remainder with decimal division.

1. Have students identify 7.0 as the dividend (number being divided) and 0.3 as the divisor (number in each set when the dividend is separated into equal groups).

2. Have students build the model of 7.0 with 7 sets of 10 studs and draw the model.

3. Ask students what brick to use to model the division based on the number of tenths in the divisor of 0.3 (answer: a 1x3 brick, since there are 3 tenths in 0.3). Ask students to model the division of 7.0 into sets of 3 tenths using 1x3 bricks. Have students draw the outline of each set of 3 studs on their drawing of the model, and label the drawing. *Note:* Make sure students understand that because each stud is 1 tenth, three studs represents 0.3.

4. Have students count the number of 1x3 bricks on the model (*answer:* 23 bricks with one stud not covered). Now that students have found the whole number portion of the solution (23), they will need to use what they know about fractions to determine the fractional part that is left over.

5. Ask students how many studs are on the 1x3 brick (*answer:* 3). Explain to students that 1 of 3 studs is $\frac{1}{3}$ of the whole brick.

6. Ask students what the one stud left over represents (*answer:* $\frac{1}{3}$ of the left over set, or the remainder).

Since we want the solution to be in decimal format, some knowledge about repeating decimals is necessary. The fractions $\frac{1}{3}$ and $\frac{2}{3}$ are interesting and easy to convert without computation. 1 x 3 = 3, so $\frac{1}{3}$ = .333; 2 x 3 = 6 so $\frac{2}{3}$ = .666 (this is not true for other decimals, but is unique to these two).

7. Ask students to explain the solution to the division problem (*answer:* 23.333 sets of 0.3 are in 7.0) and write a math sentence for the problem (*answer:* 7.0 ÷ 0.3 = 23.333).

Problem #4: Solve the division problem: 1.2 ÷ 0.2

1. Have students build a decimal grid and model the dividend of 1.2 with 1 whole strip of 10 studs and 2 additional studs, and draw the model.

2. Have students determine which brick should represent the divisor (answer: a 1x2 brick, because the divisor is 0.2). Ask students to explain their thought process to be sure they understand that the problem asks for sets of 2 tenths and each stud represents $\frac{1}{10}$ in this model.

3. Have students cover the bricks that represent 1.2 with 1x2 bricks. Have students count the number of 1x2 bricks used (*answer*: 6).

4. Have students outline the 1x2 bricks on their drawing of the model.

5. Have students write an explanation of the solution and a math sentence (*answer*: 1.2 divided into sets of 0.2 is equivalent to 6 sets of 0.2; math sentence: 1.2 ÷ 0.2 = 6).

Part 2: Show What You Know

1. Can you solve this division problem? 4.0 ÷ 0.2

    a. Build a grid model that shows the dividend.
    b. Determine the divisor brick based on the decimal of the divisor.
    c. Cover the dividend bricks with the divisor bricks.
    d. Count the number of divisor bricks used to find the solution.
    e. Write a math sentence and label your model.

Hint: The dividend will show how many 1x10 bricks to use to model that number. The divisor will show which brick to use to find the total number of wholes in the solution.

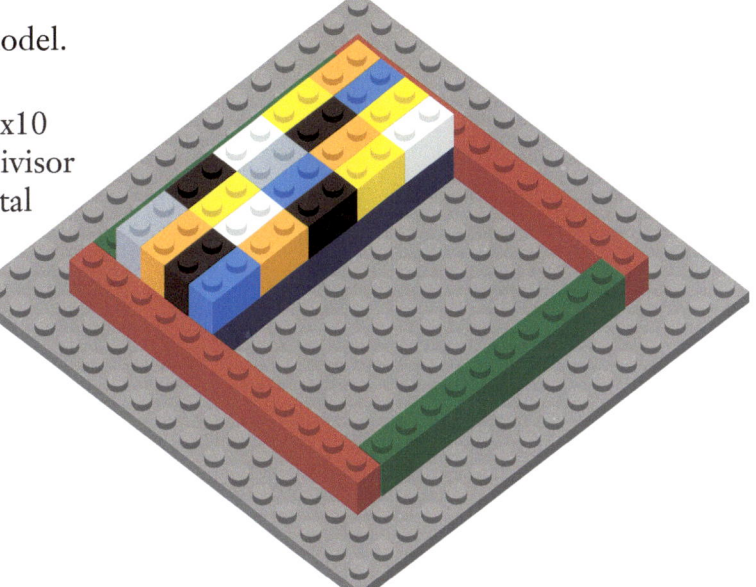

Solution:
4.0 ÷ 0.2 = 20 sets of 0.2

2. Can you solve this division problem? 5.0 ÷ 0.4

    a. Build a grid model that shows the dividend.
    b. Determine the divisor brick based on the decimal of the divisor.
    c. Cover the dividend bricks with the divisor bricks.
    d. Count the number of divisor bricks used to find the solution.
    e. Write a math sentence and label your model.

Possible solution:

1.0 divided into sets of 0.4 = 12.5 sets of 0.4
5.0 ÷ 0.4 = 12.5

3. Can you solve this division problem? 2.4 ÷ 0.2

    a. Build a grid model that shows the dividend.
    b. Determine the divisor brick based on the decimal of the divisor.
    c. Cover the dividend bricks with the divisor bricks.
    d. Count the number of divisor bricks used to find the solution.
    e. Write a math sentence and label your model.

Possible solution:

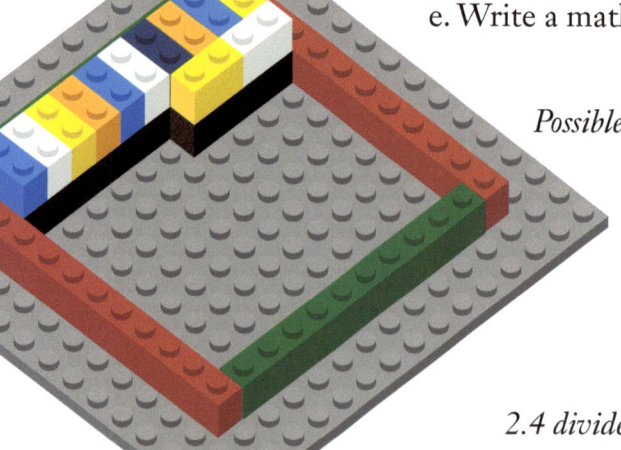

2.4 divided into sets of 0.2 = 12 sets of 0.2
2.4 ÷ 0.2 = 12

4. Can you solve this division problem? 3.5 ÷ 0.3

    a. Build a grid model that shows the dividend.
    b. Determine the divisor brick based on the decimal of the divisor.
    c. Cover the dividend bricks with the divisor bricks.
    d. Count the number of divisor bricks used to find the solution.
    e. Write a math sentence and label your model.

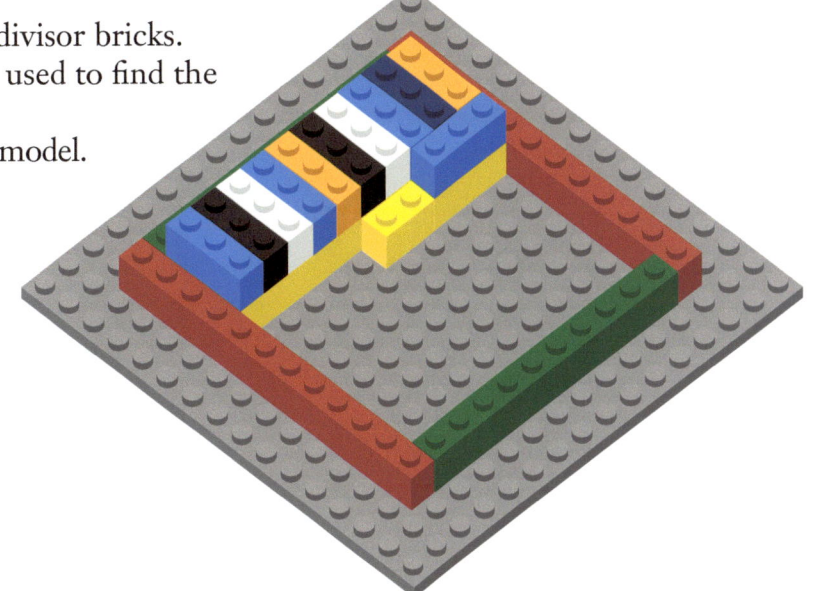

Possible solution:

3.5 divided into sets of 0.3 is equivalent to 11 sets of 0.3 and 2/3 of a set of 0.3
2/3 = 0.666
3.5 ÷ 0.3 = 11.666 sets of 0.3

SUGGESTED BRICKS

Size	Number
1x1	60
1x2	25
1x3	12
1x4	10
1x6	4
1x8	4
1x10	2
1x12	2
2x2	6
2x3	6
2x4	6

Note: Using a baseplate helps keep the bricks in place. One baseplate is suggested for these activities.

DIVIDING WHOLE AND MIXED NUMBERS BY DECIMALS USING A PLACE VALUE MODEL

Students will learn/discover:
- How to divide a whole number by a decimal value
- How to divide a mixed decimal by a decimal
- How to use a place value model to divide decimals

Why is this important?
Dividing decimals is a skill that naturally progresses from division of whole numbers, and it should be approached in the same manner. In everyday life, students will need to divide decimals when handling money or calculating time. Students should also relate the division of decimals to fractions as they learn to use equal groups with fractional parts in a decimal format.

Vocabulary:
- **Decimal number:** A number with a fractional part represented by figures to the right of a decimal point; these figures are the numerator of the equivalent fraction, whose denominator is a power of ten (e.g., the decimal .2 is equivalent to $^2/_{10}$ or $^{20}/_{100}$)
- **Decimal notation:** A representation of a fraction or other real number using the base ten system, with any of the digits 0, 1, 2, 3, 4, 5, 6, 7, 8, 9, and a decimal point

- **Mixed decimal:** A decimal value that includes a whole number and a decimal portion of another whole (e.g., 3.2 means 3 wholes and 2 tenths of another whole)
- **Tenth:** One of ten equal parts of a whole (10^{-1} or $1/10$ or .10); in decimal notation, the tenths place is the first place value position to the right of the decimal point
- **Hundredth:** One of 100 equal parts of a whole (10^{-2} or $1/100$ or .01); in decimal notation, the hundredths place is the second place value position to the right of the decimal point
- **Thousandth:** One of 1000 equal parts of a whole (10^{-3} or $1/1000$ or .001); in decimal notation, the thousandths place is the third place value position to the right of the decimal point
- **Quotitive division:** The process of repeated subtraction of the same number at each iteration
- **Partitive (equal groups) division:** The process of partitioning a given amount into equal groups
- **Quotient:** The answer to a division problem
- **Dividend:** The number being divided
- **Divisor:** The number of sets into which the dividend is being divided

How to use the companion student book, *Decimals Using LEGO® Bricks—Student Edition*:
- After students build their models, have them draw the models and explain their thinking in the Student Edition. Recording the models on paper after building them with bricks helps reinforce the concepts being taught.
- Discuss the vocabulary for each lesson with students as they work through the Student Edition.
- Use the chapter assessments in the Student Edition to gauge student understanding of the content.

Part 1: Show Them How

Review the definition of a decimal and what it represents (*answer:* like a fraction, a decimal is a form of notation used to represent a part of a whole). *Note:* It is important that students make the connection between decimal and fractional representations of parts of a whole.

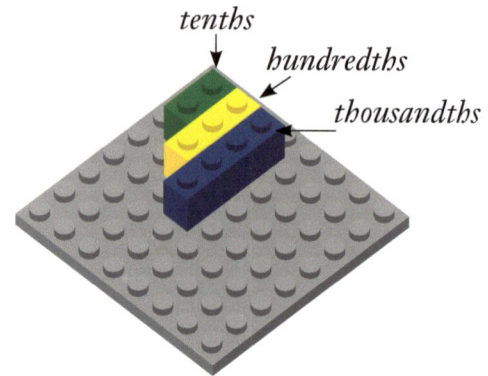

Review the definition of division as the breaking apart of a number into equal groups. The process of division can thought of in two ways: as *partitive*, where a given amount is partitioned into equal groups (also called *equal groups* division); and *quotitive*, where *repeated subtraction* is used to find the number of sets.

Explain to students that division of decimals follows the same general practice as division of fractions: the quotient is usually larger than the dividend or the divisor because the quotient refers to groups or sets.

If needed, review with students how to model the base ten decimal system with bricks.

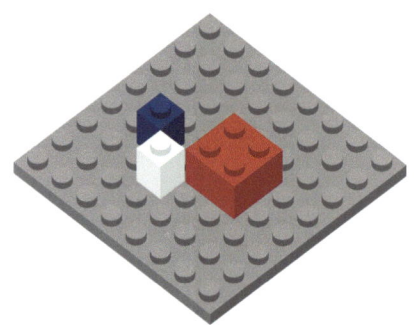

1 whole and 2 tenths
1.2

Use a 1x1 brick to model the decimal point, one row below the bricks modeling the numbers. It is helpful to use the same color to represent the decimal point each time. As an example, model 1.2, and have students create the same model.

Review with students how to decompose. As a way to visualize decomposing, ask students how many pennies are in one dime (*answer:* 10). Remind students that this shows that "10 tenths" is the same as "1 whole."

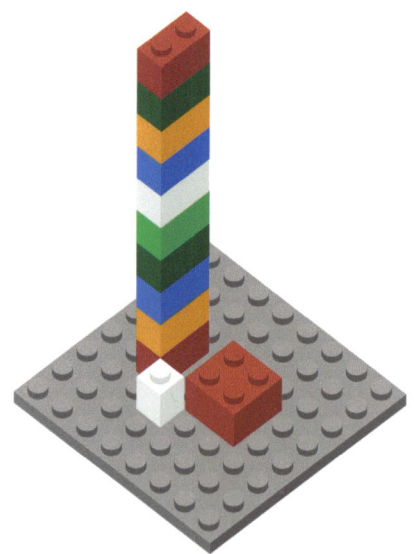

1 whole decomposed into 10 sets of $1/10$

Using the model of 1.2, have students decompose the 1 whole into 10 tenths by replacing the 1x1 brick with ten 1x2 bricks.

80   DECIMALS USING LEGO® BRICKS—TEACHER EDITION | DR. SHIRLEY DISSELER

Combine all the tenths by stacking them to the right of the decimal point. There will be 12 tenths in the stack.

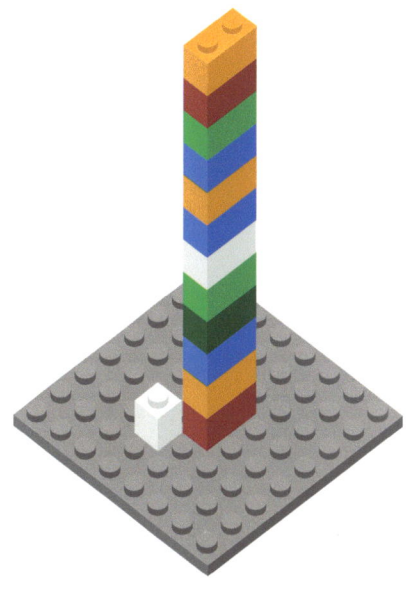

10 tenths and 2 tenths combined

Problem #1: Solve the division problem: 1.2 ÷ 0.2

1. Ask students what question this problem is asking (*answer:* How many sets of 0.2 are in 1.2?).

2. Ask students how to model 0.2 (answer: two 1x2 bricks). Using the decomposed model of 1.2 just created, divide it into sets of 0.2. Have students divide the stack of twelve 1x2 bricks into equal groups of two 1x2 bricks each.

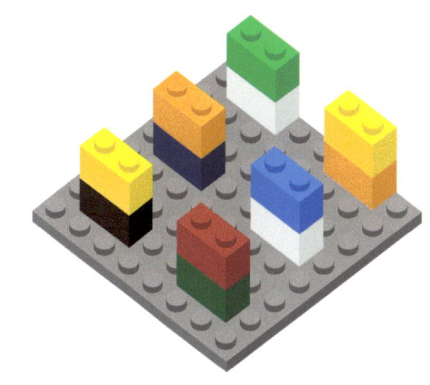

3. The model shows 12 tenths divided into 6 sets of 2 tenths. The solution to the problem: 1.2 ÷ 0.2 = 6

Problem #2: Solve the division problem: 2.0 ÷ 0.25
Note: It is helpful to have students think of the problem as "How many quarters ($0.25) will make two dollars ($2.00)?"

1. Build a place value model of the dividend, 2.0. Decompose the 2 wholes into two sets of 10 tenths, or 20 tenths, modeling them with twenty 1x2 bricks.

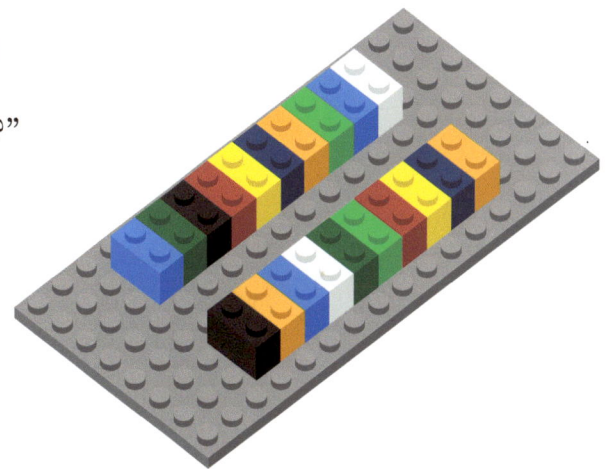

Note: Explain to students that 20 tenths (or 20 dimes) is equal to 200 hundredths (or 200 pennies). One dollar is worth 100 pennies, so one whole is equivalent to 100 hundredths.

2. Use set division from the whole number method to find the number of sets of 25 in 200.

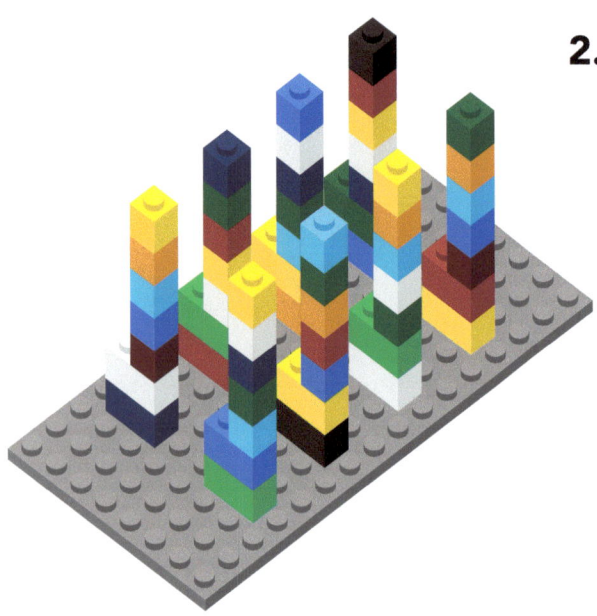

Make equal groups of 25 from the bricks modeling 200. To do so, decompose one 1x2 brick into ten 1x3 bricks, then model each group of 25 by stacking two 1x2 bricks and five 1x3 bricks. Four 1x2 bricks will be decomposed into forty 1x3 bricks to provide enough bricks to divide all the bricks into eight equal groups. *Note:* 1x1 bricks can be used instead of 1x3 bricks to show the hundredths place value brick if you do not have forty 1x3 bricks. 1x1 bricks are shown in the illustration.

2.00 divided into sets of 0.25 is 8 sets of 0.25.

Note: Students should always quantify the numerical answer by stating it in terms of sets; here, "sets of 0.25."

Problem #3: Solve the division problem: 1.25 ÷ 0.5

1. Have students write what the problem is asking (*answer:* 1 whole and 25 hundredths divided into sets of 5 tenths). Make sure students understand that the problem is asking how many equal groups of 5 tenths are in 1 whole and 25 hundredths. Have students think about it in terms of money; i. e., converting $1.25 into sets of 5 dimes.

2. Build a place value model of 1.25. Have students build the same model. Explain to students that the problem can also be viewed as 125 pennies (125 hundredths or $1.25) being divided into sets of 5 dimes.

3. Decompose the 1 whole into 10 tenths (ten 1x2 bricks).

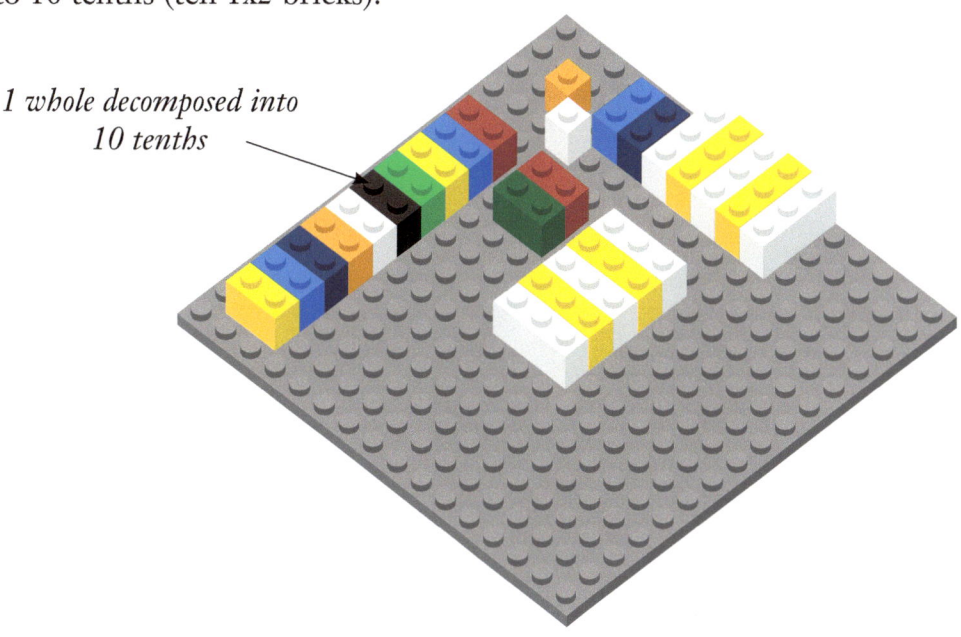

1 whole decomposed into 10 tenths

4. Divide the ten 1x2 bricks into groups representing 5 tenths (five 1x2 bricks). Students should see that the ten 1x2 bricks divide evenly into two groups of five 1x2 bricks.

The bricks that are left over model 0.25, which is exactly half of 0.5. Therefore, the bricks have been divided into 2½ groups of 5 tenths, or 2.5 groups of 5 tenths.

The solution is: 2.5 sets of 0.5 are in 1.25.

1.25 ÷ 0.5 = 2.5

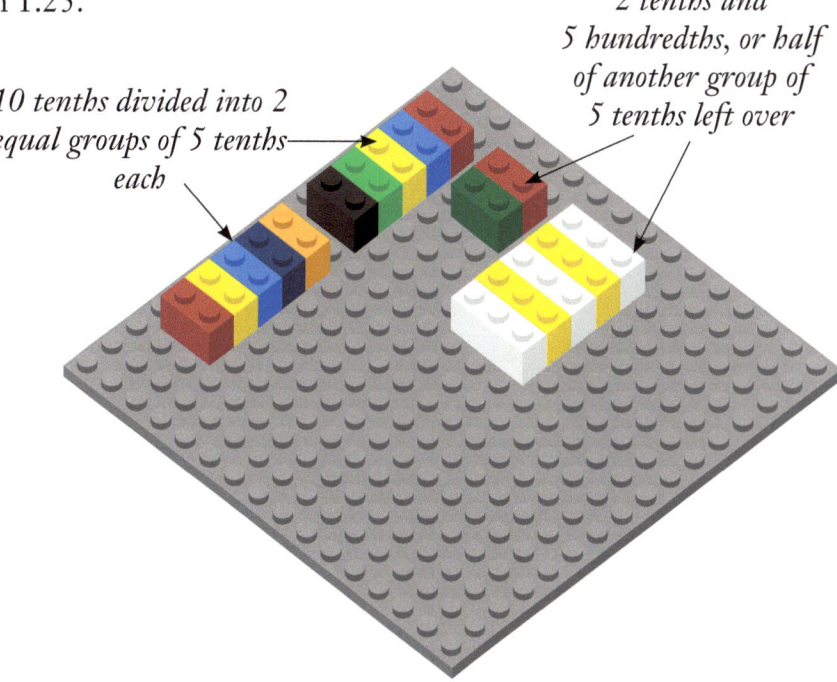

10 tenths divided into 2 equal groups of 5 tenths each

2 tenths and 5 hundredths, or half of another group of 5 tenths left over

DR. SHIRLEY DISSELER | DECIMALS USING LEGO® BRICKS—TEACHER EDITION

Part 2: Show What You Know

1. Can you solve this division problem? 1.4 ÷ 0.2
   a. Build a model of 1.4
   b. Decompose the 1 whole into 10 tenths
   c. Divide all the tenths into even groups of 2 tenths each

Answer: 1.4 ÷ 0.2 = 7 groups of 0.2

Possible solution:

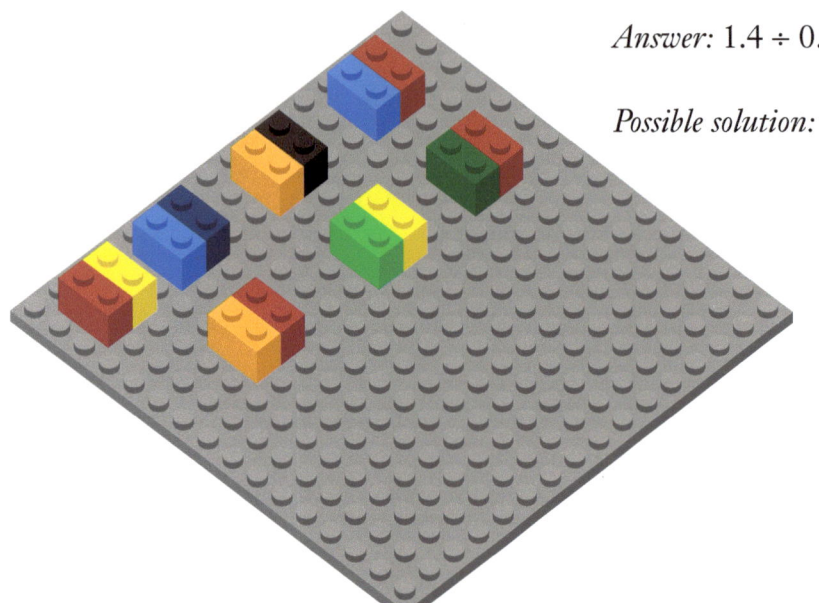

14 tenths divided into
7 equal groups of
2 tenths each

2. Can you solve this division problem? 2.4 ÷ 0.3
   a. Build a model of 2.4
   b. Decompose the 2 wholes into 20 tenths
   c. Divide all the tenths into even groups of 3 tenths each

Answer: 2.4 ÷ 0.3 = 8 groups of 0.3

Possible solution:

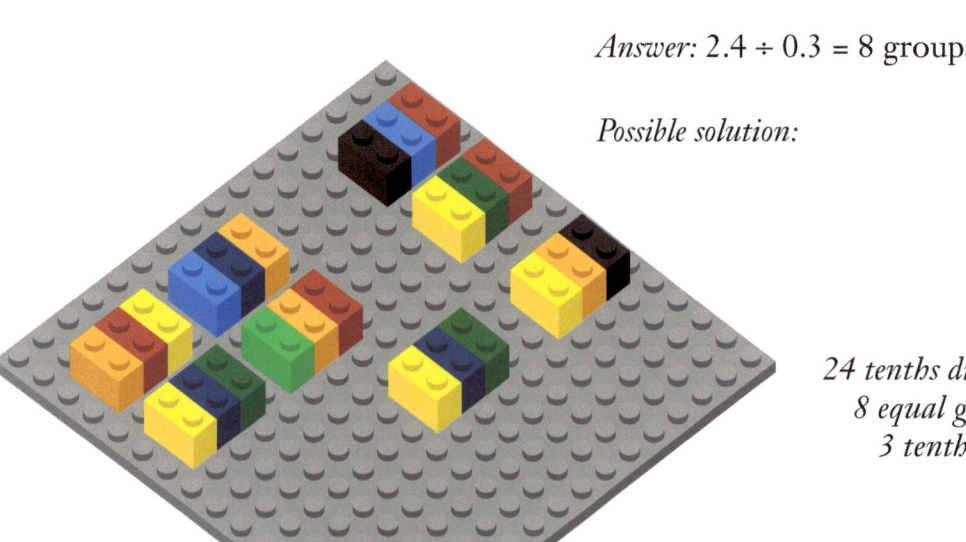

24 tenths divided into
8 equal groups of
3 tenths each

3. Can you solve this division problem? 2.8 ÷ 0.2
   a. Build a model of 2.8
   b. Decompose the 2 wholes into 20 tenths
   c. Divide all the tenths into even groups of 2 tenths each

Answer: 2.8 ÷ 0.2 = 14 groups of 0.2

Possible solution:

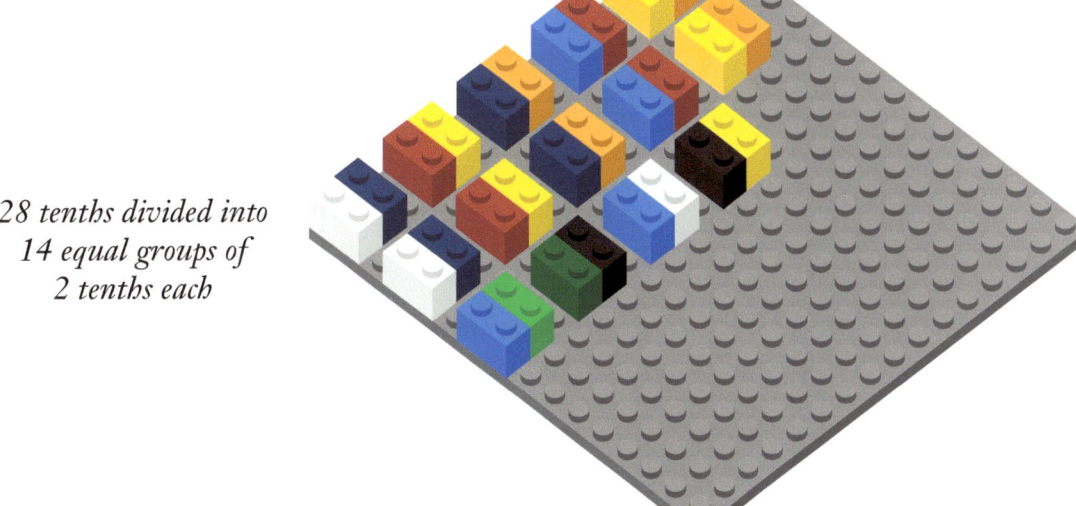

place value model of 2.8

2 wholes decomposed into 20 tenths

28 tenths divided into 14 equal groups of 2 tenths each

DR. SHIRLEY DISSELER | DECIMALS USING LEGO® BRICKS—TEACHER EDITION

9

SUGGESTED BRICKS

Size	Number
1x1	60
1x2	25
1x3	12
1x4	10
1x6	4
1x8	4
1x10	2
1x12	2
2x2	6
2x3	6
2x4	6

Note: Using a baseplate helps keep the bricks in place. One baseplate is suggested for these activities.

DIVIDING BY DECIMALS USING A GRID COVERING STRATEGY

Students will learn/discover:
- How to divide a mixed decimal by a decimal
- How to divide a decimal by a decimal
- How to divide a whole number by a decimal
- How to model the division of decimals using a grid covering strategy
- How to interpret an "equal groups" model to divide decimals

Why is this important?
Dividing decimals is a skill that naturally progresses from division of whole numbers and should be approached in the same manner. In everyday life, students will need to divide decimals when handling money or calculating time. Students should also relate the division of decimals to fractions as they learn to use equal groups with fractional parts in a decimal format.

Vocabulary:
- **Decimal number:** A number with a fractional part represented by figures to the right of a decimal point; these figures are the numerator of the equivalent fraction, whose denominator is a power of ten (e.g., the decimal .2 is equivalent to $^2/_{10}$ or $^{20}/_{100}$)

- **Decimal notation:** A representation of a fraction or other real number using the base ten system, with any of the digits 0, 1, 2, 3, 4, 5, 6, 7, 8, 9, and a decimal point
- **Mixed decimal:** A whole number combined with a decimal part of another whole (e.g., 3.2 means 3 wholes and 2 tenths of another whole)
- **Tenth:** One of ten equal parts of a whole (10^{-1} or $1/10$ or .10); in decimal notation, the tenths place is the first place value position to the right of the decimal point
- **Hundredth:** One of 100 equal parts of a whole (10^{-2} or $1/100$ or .01); in decimal notation, the hundredths place is the second place value position to the right of the decimal point
- **Thousandth:** One of 1000 equal parts of a whole (10^{-3} or $1/1000$ or .001); in decimal notation, the thousandths place is the third place value position to the right of the decimal point
- **Quotitive division:** The process of repeated subtraction of the same number at each iteration
- **Partitive (equal groups) division:** The partitioning of a given amount into equal groups
- **Quotient:** The answer to a division problem
- **Dividend:** The number being divided
- **Divisor:** The number of sets into which the dividend is being divided

How to use the companion student book, *Decimals Using LEGO® Bricks—Student Edition*:
- After students build their models, have them draw the models and explain their thinking in the Student Edition. Recording the models on paper after building them with bricks helps reinforce the concepts being taught.
- Discuss the vocabulary for each lesson with students as they work through the Student Edition.
- Use the chapter assessments in the Student Edition to gauge student understanding of the content.

Part 1: Show Them How

Note: Computationally, when dividing decimals in the base ten system, the divisor and dividend are multiplied by the power of 10 that it takes to make the divisor a whole number. This idea can be modeled using the "grid covering" method:

1. Model the dividend in a 100-stud grid, with each stud representing .01.

2. Model the divisor with a second layer of bricks in which each stud represents 0.1. In the grid covering method, the value of the divisor indicates the size brick to use in this second layer (e.g., a divisor of 0.2 means that 1x2 bricks should be used). Cover the dividend layer entirely with this size brick.

3. Multiply the number of studs in the brick that represents the divisor by 10 (i.e., the power of 10 that it takes to make the divisor a whole number). This shows the number of studs in each set of the divisor in the solution (e.g., a 1x2 brick has 2 studs; 2 x 10 = 20; there are 20 studs in each set of the divisor in the solution).

Note: This grid covering method works only when the divisor is a decimal in tenths.

The bricks used to cover the bricks that model the dividend will be as follows for the problems in this chapter:

1x2 brick for a divisor of 0.2

1x3 brick for a divisor of 0.3

In this way, a set of 10 bricks represents 1 whole set of the divisor.

Problem #1: Solve 0.8 ÷ 0.2

1. Build a decimal grid and cover 80 studs, representing 0.8. *Note:* Each 1x10 column of bricks represents one tenth, and there are 8 of them in the grid to represent 0.8.

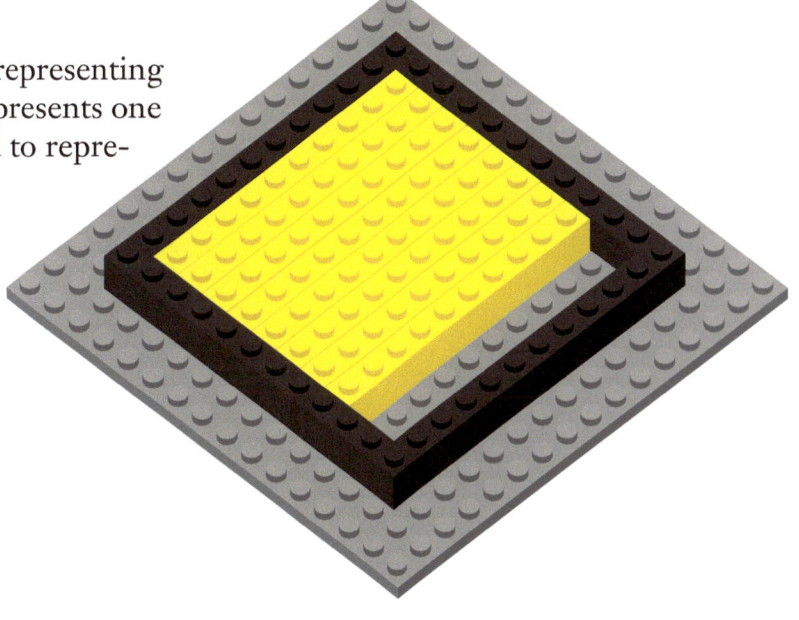

2. Ask students how to model the problem of 8 tenths divided into sets of 2 tenths (*answer:* cover the bricks in the grid that model 8 tenths with a layer of 1x2 bricks). Cover the bricks that model 8 tenths with a layer of four sets of ten 1x2 bricks in different colors (use two 1x1 bricks if you don't have enough 1x2 bricks).

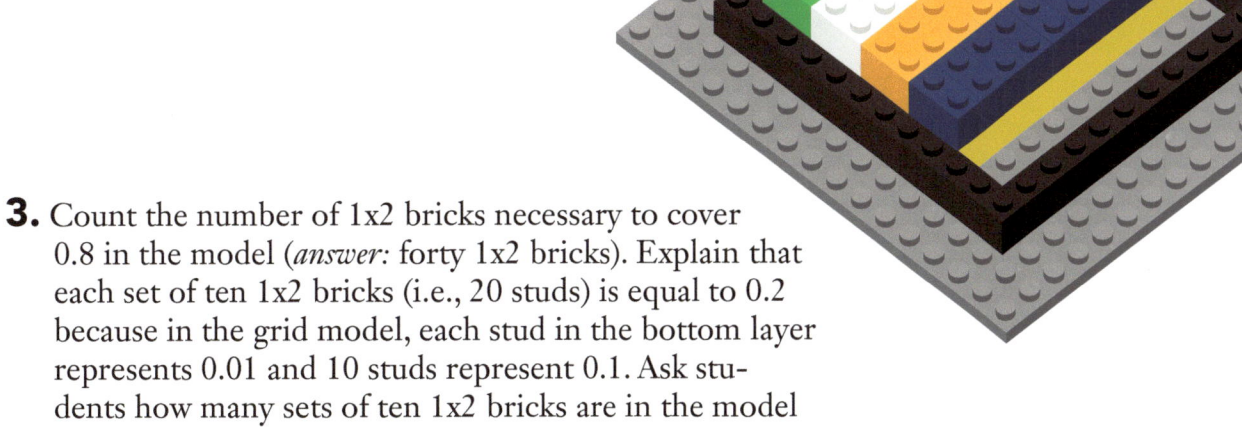

3. Count the number of 1x2 bricks necessary to cover 0.8 in the model (*answer:* forty 1x2 bricks). Explain that each set of ten 1x2 bricks (i.e., 20 studs) is equal to 0.2 because in the grid model, each stud in the bottom layer represents 0.01 and 10 studs represent 0.1. Ask students how many sets of ten 1x2 bricks are in the model (*answer:* 4 sets).

4. Have students write a math sentence for the solution (*answer:* 0.8 ÷ 0.2 = 4 sets of 0.2).

5. Have students draw the model and outline the sets on the top layer of the model.

Problem #2: Build a grid model to show 0.54 ÷ 0.3 and write a math sentence for the solution.

0.54

1. Build a decimal grid and cover 54 studs, representing 0.54.

   Note: Make sure students understand that each stud in the grid represents 0.01.

2. Ask students which brick can be used to represent 0.3 (*answer:* 1x3 brick) and why (*answer:* because the 1x3 brick on the top layer represents a divisor of 0.3).

3. Have students cover the original model with a layer of 1x3 bricks, and count the number of 1x3 bricks used (*answer:* eighteen 1x3 bricks).

4. In this problem, since the divisor is 0.3, each set of 30 studs is 1 whole set. Ask students how many 1x3 bricks are equal to 1 whole set (*answer:* ten 1x3 bricks, because 3 studs x 10 = 30 studs).

   Since there are eighteen 1x3 bricks in the top layer of the model, there are 8 tenths left over. That makes the solution 1 whole and 8 tenths.

5. Write a math sentence for the solution (*answer:* 0.54 ÷ 0.3 = 1 whole and 8 tenths = 1.8 sets of 0.3).

Problem #3: Solve 1.75 ÷ 0.25

Note: It may be helpful for students to think of this problem in terms of money: $1.75 divided into sets of 25 cents.

Note: In this problem, the divisor of 0.25 is represented by sets of 25 studs. Because the divisor is already a decimal in the hundredths place, multiplication by 10 is not required (i.e., the top and bottom layers of the model are both in terms of hundredths already).

1. Build a decimal grid model for 1.0 by covering all 100 studs in the decimal grid.

2. Add 0.75 to the model, by covering the space around the decimal grid with three sets of 25 studs, each representing 0.25. It will be clearer to students if each set of 25 studs outside the grid is created with a different color brick. *Note:* This step will require some creativity. One possible arrangement is illustrated.

   0.25 (25 studs)

   0.25 (25 studs)

   1.0 (100 studs)

   0.25 (25 studs)

3. Model the number of sets of 0.25 in 1.75 by covering the bottom layer of bricks in and around the decimal grid with sets of 25 studs. If possible, create each set of 25 studs in the top layer with a different color of brick.

4. Identify the total number of sets of 0.25 (or 25 studs) on the baseplate (*answer:* 7 sets). Write a math sentence for the solution (*answer:* 1.75 ÷ 0.25 = 7).

Part 2: Show What You Know

1. Can you build a grid model to show 0.62 ÷ 0.2, or the number of sets of 0.2 in 0.62, by covering the bricks that model the dividend?

Draw your model and explain your thinking, and write a math sentence for the solution.

Possible solution:

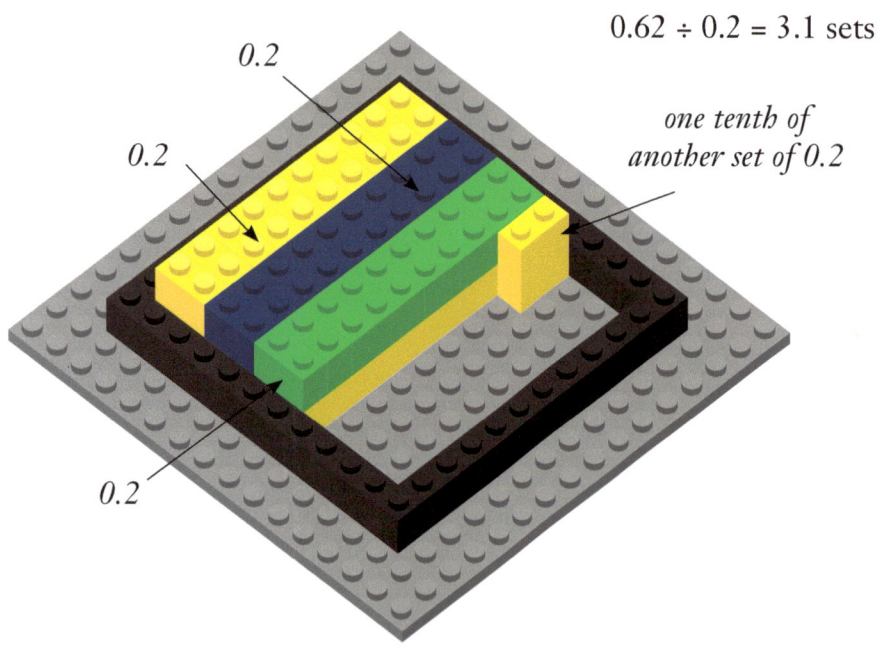

model of 0.62

Each set of 0.2 is represented by ten 1x2 bricks (20 studs). Three sets of 0.2 and 0.1 of another set of 0.2 (one 1x2 brick) cover 0.62 in the model.

0.62 ÷ 0.2 = 3.1 sets of 0.2

0.62 divided by 3.1 sets of 0.2

92   DECIMALS USING LEGO® BRICKS—TEACHER EDITION | DR. SHIRLEY DISSELER

2. Can you build a model to show 1.4 ÷ 0.7, or the number of sets of 0.7 in 1.4, using the grid covering strategy?

Draw your model and explain your thinking, and write a math sentence for the solution.

Possible solution:

*model of 1.4
(1 whole and 4 tenths)*

Each set of 0.7 is represented by 70 studs. Two sets of 0.7 cover 1.4 in the model.

1.4 ÷ 0.7 = 2

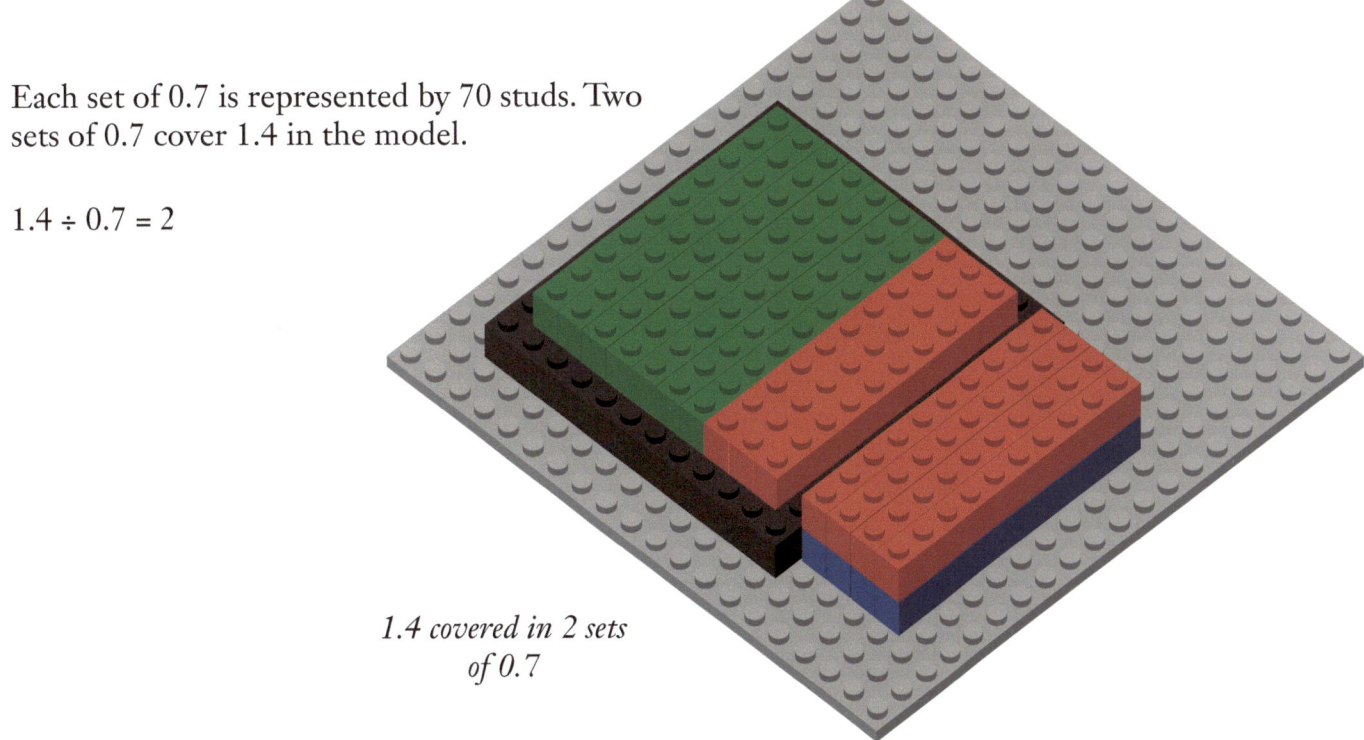

*1.4 covered in 2 sets
of 0.7*

3. Can you build a model to show 0.45 ÷ 0.3 using the grid covering strategy? Draw the model of 0.45 and then outline sets of 0.3 in your model. Explain your thinking and write a math sentence for your model.

Possible solution:

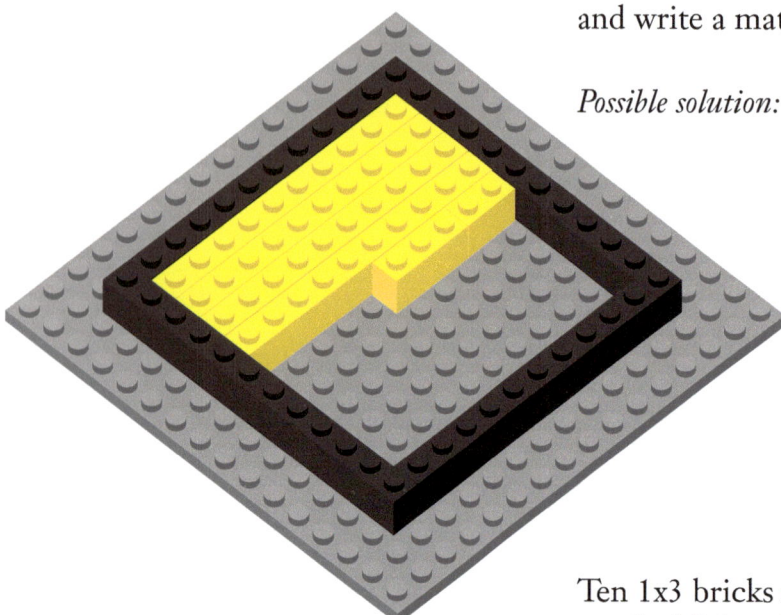

model of 0.45

Ten 1x3 bricks represent 1 whole set of 0.3, and there are 5 additional 1x3 bricks, or one-half of a set of 0.3, so the solution is 1.5 sets of 0.3.

Math sentence: 0.45 ÷ 0.3 = 1.5

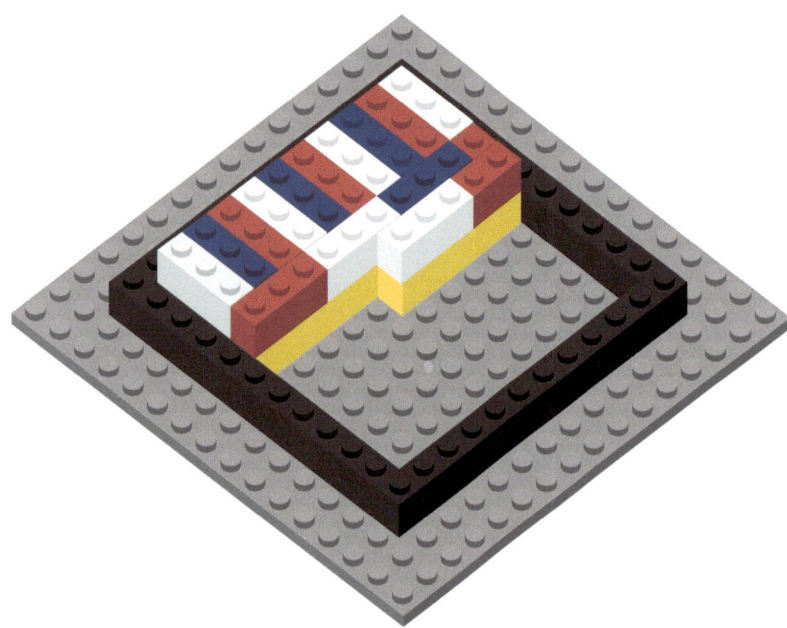

15 sets of 1x3 bricks covering 45 studs

LINKING DECIMALS, FRACTIONS, AND PERCENTAGES

SUGGESTED BRICKS

Size	Number
1x1	24
1x2	25
1x3	12
1x4	10
1x6	4
1x8	4
1x10	6
1x12	2
2x2	6
2x3	6
2x4	9
2x6	4
2x8	2
2x10	2

Note: Using a baseplate helps keep the bricks in place. One baseplate is suggested for these activities.

Students will learn/discover:
- How to find a percent of a whole
- How to write an amount as a fraction, decimal, and percentage
- How to find the percent of a given amount in a word problem

Why is this important?
Real-world situations require students to understand how percentages are linked to fractional and decimal parts, and how the same number can be written as a fraction, decimal, and percentage. Students need to understand the relationship between percentages, fractions, and decimals in order to solve many problems involving parts of a group, money and economics, graphing and data analysis, and much more.

Vocabulary:
- **Decimal number:** A number with a fractional part represented by figures to the right of a decimal point; these figures are the numerator of the equivalent fraction, whose denominator is a power of ten (e.g., the decimal .2 is equivalent to $^2/_{10}$ or $^{20}/_{100}$)
- **Decimal notation:** A representation of a fraction or other real number using the base ten system, with any of the digits 0, 1, 2, 3, 4, 5, 6, 7, 8, 9, and a decimal point
- **Percent:** Like a fraction and a decimal, a percent is a form of notation used to represent a part of a whole; one part of every one hundred is equal to 1 percent (1%)

How to use the companion student book, *Decimals Using LEGO® Bricks–Student Edition*:

- After students build their models, have them draw the models and explain their thinking in the Student Edition. Recording the models on paper after building them with bricks helps reinforce the concepts being taught.
- Discuss the vocabulary for each lesson with students as they work through the Student Edition.
- Use the chapter assessments in the Student Edition to gauge student understanding of the content.

Part 1: Show Them How

Note: In middle school, students will need to know how to use computational models to find the percent of a given amount. Typically, computational models are taught using ratios (e.g., ¾ is equivalent to the ratio 3:4, which is then translated into a percentage). In this chapter, however, these problems will be solved by visualizing tenths of a whole in two different ways. First, students will use the decimal grid model to determine percentages by visualizing tenths as strips of 10 studs in a 10 x 10 decimal grid. Then, students will use a "tenths model" to determine percentages by dividing groups of studs on a baseplate by 10.

Review how to model decimal amounts using the decimal grid model (see Chapter 1).

Review the definition of a decimal and what it represents (*answer:* like a fraction, a decimal is a form of notation used to represent a part of a whole). *Note:* It is important that students make the connection between decimal and fractional representations of parts of a whole.

Review the definition of a percent (*answer:* a percent is used to represent part of a whole; one part of every one hundred is 1 percent).

Ask students how percents are related to fractions and decimals (*answer:* all three represent parts of a whole).

Fraction: part of a whole

Decimal: part of a whole (fraction) whose denominator is part of the base ten system

Percent: part of a whole (fraction) represented "per 100," or out of 100

Explain that this lesson will involve building models to show fractions, decimals, and percents.

Problem #1: Cover a grid model with 30 studs. Draw it and label the studs covered as a fraction, decimal, and percent.

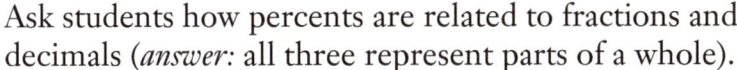
3 sets of 10 studs

1. Build a grid model and cover 30 studs, or 3 sets of 10 studs.

2. Ask students how to write this amount as a fraction (*answer:* since each set of 10 studs is $1/10$, three sets of 10 is the fraction $3/10$).

3. Ask students how to write this amount as a decimal (*answer:* 0.3). *Note:* Review how to use the numerator and denominator to find the place value of the decimal (*answer:* the denominator [tenths] signals the place value of the numerator [3] in the decimal [0.3]).

4. Ask students how to write this amount as a percent (*answer:* since each stud represents 1 percentage point of 100 percent, 30 studs covered equals 30% of the grid). Draw the model and write the fraction, decimal, and percent modeled (*answer:* fraction: $3/10$; decimal: 0.3; percent: 30%).

Note: Problems 2 – 4 apply the concept of percents to real-world situations.

Problem #2: On sale, a TV set is selling for 30% off the original price of 100 dollars. How much does the TV cost with the discount, and how do you know?

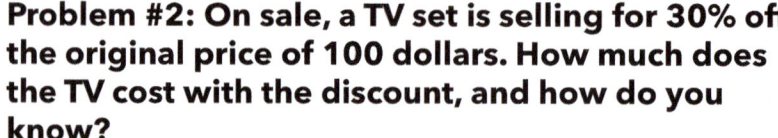

30%

1. Build a grid model to show the amount of the discount (30%). Have students build the same model.

2. Write the amount of the discount as a decimal and a fraction (*answer*: fraction = $^{30}/_{100}$ or $^{3}/_{10}$; decimal = 0.3). Explain that these are equivalent mathematical terms.

3. Explain that the 100 total studs of the decimal grid represents 100%, as well as the $100 original cost of the TV. Each stud is 1% of the whole, or 1 of 100 dollars. Count the number of uncovered studs left in the grid, and name the percent and dollar amount (*answer*: 70 studs = 70%; the discounted TV costs $70).

4. Identify the fractional and decimal equivalents of 70% (*answer*: fraction = $^{70}/_{100}$ or $^{7}/_{10}$; decimal = 0.7). Ask students how much the TV costs on sale (*answer*: $70). Draw the model and write a sentence stating the solution (*answer*: 30% of $100 equals $30. $100 minus $30 equals $70, which is the discounted price of the TV).

Problem #3: 40% of the students in the class like chocolate ice cream. If there are 30 students in the class, how many students like chocolate ice cream?

Note: Because this problem requires calculating 40% of 30 students, not 40% of 100, an approach other than the decimal grid model is needed. Instead, students should use a tenths model, which involves breaking the total number of students (30) into tenths.

1. Model the 30 students in the class by placing bricks totaling 30 studs on a baseplate. Use bricks all of one color, if possible.

98 DECIMALS USING LEGO® BRICKS—TEACHER EDITION | DR. SHIRLEY DISSELER

2. Guide students to identify the size brick to represent one tenth of 30. Have students find 10 bricks of the same size that can be used to cover the 30 studs, and identify the brick size (*answer*: 1x3 brick). Explain that they can divide 30 studs by 10 bricks to identify the brick that represents one tenth of 30 students (*answer*: 30 ÷ 10 = 3 studs or students = one 1x3 brick).

3. Ask students what percentage of the total students are represented by one 1x3 brick, if that 1x3 brick equals one tenth of the total students (*answer*: 10% of the total students).

4. Ask students if 40% (or 4 tenths) of the students like chocolate ice cream, how many sets of 10% (or 1 tenth) like chocolate ice cream (*answer*: 4 sets of 10% or 4 tenths). Place four 1x3 bricks on top of the layer of 30 studs in the model.

5. Count the number of studs covered by 1x3 bricks to find the number of students who like chocolate ice cream (*answer*: 12 studs, representing 12 students). Ask students what fraction and what percentage of the students like chocolate ice cream (*answer*: $^{12}/_{30}$ = 40%). Draw the model and write a sentence stating the solution (*answer*: 40% of 30 students equals 12 students who like chocolate ice cream).

Note: Students may alternatively place ten 1x3 bricks on top of the 30 studs that represent 30 students, and then remove six of the 1x3 bricks, leaving four 1x3 bricks (40%) in the top layer.

Problem #4: There are 80 students in the fifth grade. 25% of them ride a bus to school. How many students ride a bus to school?

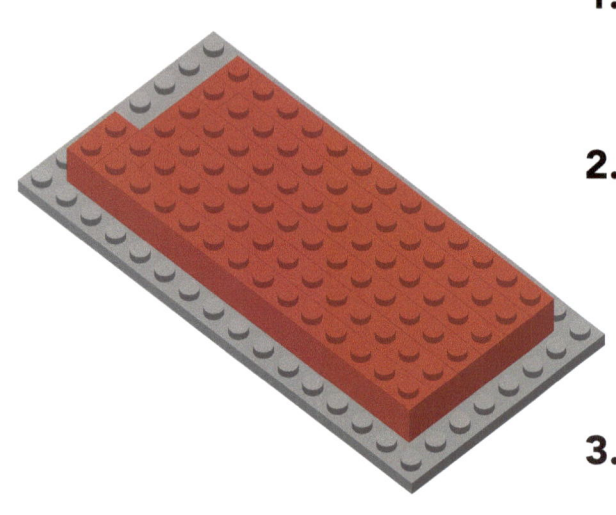

1. Use a tenths model to show 80 students who ride the bus, by placing bricks totaling 80 studs on a baseplate. Have students build the model along with you.

2. Use division to find 10% of 80 studs (*answer:* 80 ÷ 10 = 8 studs). This gives the size brick that will represent one tenth of the total 80 students. *Note:* If division is difficult for students, ask how many times 10 can be subtracted from 80. See *Division Using LEGO® Bricks—Teacher Edition*.

3. Ask students which size brick can be used to model one tenth of 80 (*answer:* a 2x4 brick or a 1x8 brick, each equal to one tenth or 10% of 80 studs).

4. Ask students how many 2x4 or 1x8 bricks equal 20% of the whole (*answer:* two 2x4 bricks, since each 2x4 brick is one tenth or 10%). Have students place two 2x4 bricks on top of the original layer of bricks. *Note:* Alternatively, students may first place the ten 8-stud bricks on top of the original layer of bricks, if they need help visualizing the percentages (use two 2x2 bricks if there are not enough 2x4 bricks). Then they would remove eight 2x4 bricks from the model, leaving two 2x4 bricks (20%) in the top layer.

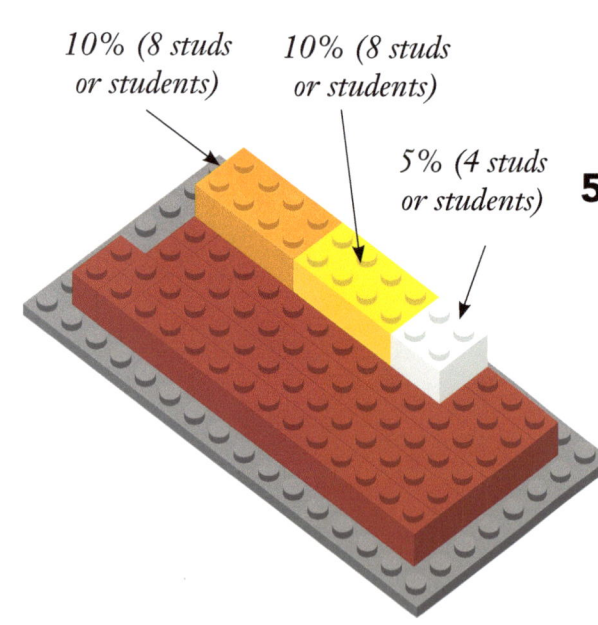

10% (8 studs or students)
10% (8 studs or students)
5% (4 studs or students)

5. Ask students how many 2x4 bricks equal 5% of the whole (*answer:* half of a 2x4 brick, since each 2x4 brick is one tenth or 10%). Add a third 2x4 brick to the model, then replace it with two 2x2 bricks. Remove one 2x2 brick to show 5%, or half of 10%.

6. Have students count the total number of studs in the top layer of the model (*answer:* 20 studs). Draw the model and write a sentence stating the solution (*answer:* 25% of 80 students equals 20 students who ride the bus to school).

Part 2: Show What You Know

1. Sarah needs to buy a printer that normally costs $100. Today it is 40% off. Can you build a decimal grid model to show the discount? Draw and label your model, and explain how you know the final cost.

Solution:

The inside of the 10 x 10 grid represents 100 dollars (1 stud = 1 dollar). Since 1 percent is 1 of 100, 40% = $^{40}/_{100}$ studs (or dollars).

100 total studs - 40 studs covered = 60 uncovered studs. The discounted printer costs $60.

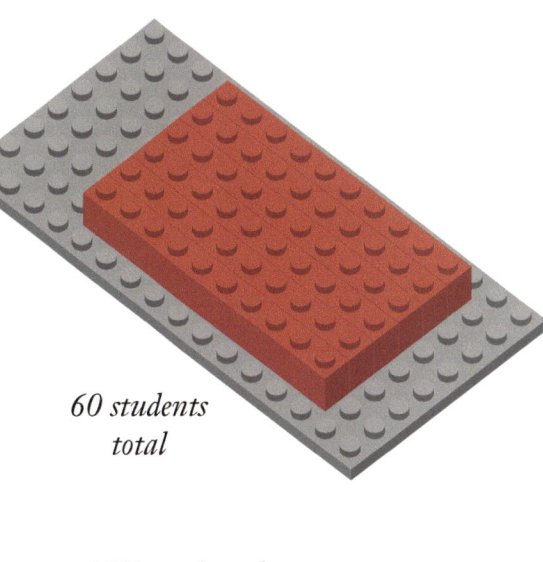

2. There are 60 students on a bus to the zoo. 15% of them are wearing tennis shoes. Can you use a tenths model to find out how many students are wearing tennis shoes? Draw and label your model, and explain how you know the number of students wearing tennis shoes.

Solution:

10% of 60 students = 60 ÷ 10 = 6 students (or studs)

5% of 60 students = half of 10% = half of 6 students = 3 students (or studs)

15% of 60 students = 6 students + 3 students = 9 students

There are 9 students wearing tennis shoes on the bus to the zoo.

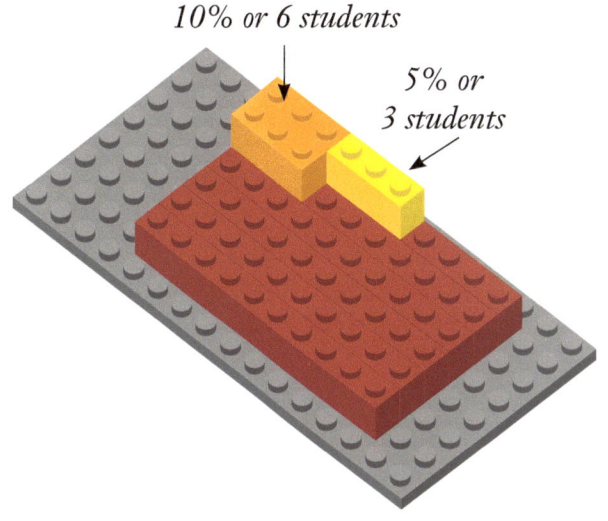

60 students total

10% or 6 students

5% or 3 students

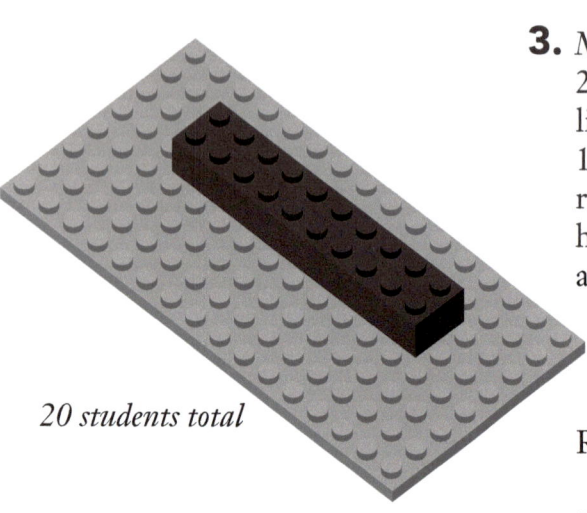

20 students total

3. Maria's teacher did a class survey about favorite colors. 20 students took the survey, which asked whether they liked red, blue, yellow, or green best. The results were: 10% liked green, 5% liked red, 25% liked blue, and the rest liked yellow. Can you build a tenths model to show how many liked each color? Draw and label your model, and explain your solution.

Green: 10% of 20 students = 20 ÷ 10 = 2 students

Red: 5% = half of 10% = half of 2 students = 1 student

Blue: 20% = twice 10% = twice 2 students = 4 students; 5% = 1 student; 25% is 4 + 1 = 5 students

Yellow: 20 students - 2 students - 1 student - 5 students = 12 students

2 students like green, 1 likes red, 5 like blue, and 12 like yellow.

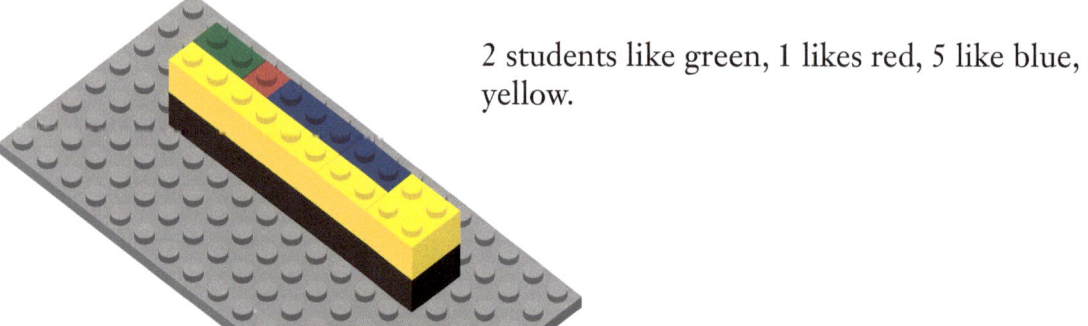

APPENDIX

- **Suggested Brick Inventory**
- **Student Assessment Chart**
- **Baseplate Paper**

SUGGESTED BRICK INVENTORY

SIZE	NUMBER
1x1	84 (32 each of two colors and 10 each of two more colors)
1x2	25 (10 each of two colors and 5 of a third color)
1x3	12 (6 each of two colors)
1x4	10
1x6	10
1x8	6
1x10	6
1x12	5
1x16	2
2x2	12
2x3	6
2x4	9
2x6	4
2x8	2
2x10	2

DECIMALS
Student Assessment Chart

Name _____

Performance Skill	Not yet	With help	On target	Comments
I can model and explain the meaning of a decimal.				
I can model and explain the place value of the digits in a decimal.				
I can model and explain how to use a grid model to show a decimal amount.				
I can model and explain expanded form of a decimal.				
I can model and explain addition and subtraction of decimals.				
I can model and explain multiplication of decimals.				
I can model and explain division of decimals.				
I can relate decimals to fractions and percentages.				

BASEPLATE PAPER

BASEPLATE PAPER

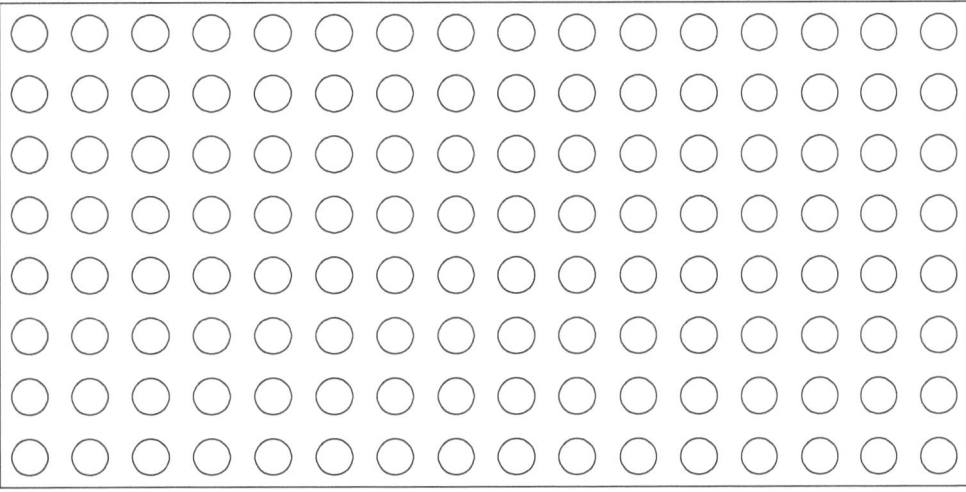

www.ingramcontent.com/pod-product-compliance
Lightning Source LLC
Chambersburg PA
CBHW041700160426
43191CB00002B/35